Quiet Talks on Power

Quiet Talks on Power

S. D. GORDON

THE FAMILY INSPIRATIONAL LIBRARY

PUBLISHERS *Grosset & Dunlap* NEW YORK

1978 Printing
ISBN 0-448-01656-7
PRINTED IN THE UNITED STATES OF AMERICA

Contents

Quiet Talks on Power

Choked

Channels

An Odd Distinction

A few years ago I was making a brief tour among the colleges of Missouri. I remember one morning in a certain college village going over from the hotel to take breakfast with some of the boys, and coming back with one of the fellows whom I had just met. As we walked along, chatting away, I asked him quietly, "Are you a christian, sir?" He turned quickly and looked at me with an odd, surprised expression in his eye and then turning his face away said: "Well, I'm a member of church, but—I don't believe I'm very much of a christian." Then I looked at him and he frankly volunteered a little information. Not very much. He did not need to say much. You can see a large field through a chink in the fence. And I saw enough to let me know that he was right in the criticism he had made upon himself. We talked a bit and parted. But his remark set me to thinking.

A week later, in another town, speaking one morning to the students of a young ladies' seminary, I said afterwards to one of the teachers as we were talking: "I suppose your young women here are all christians." That same quizzical look came into her eye as she said: "I think they are all members of church, but I do not think they are all christians with real power in their lives." There was that same odd distinction.

A few weeks later, in Kansas City visiting the medical and dental schools, I recall distinctly standing one morning in a disordered room— shavings on the floor, desks disarranged—the institution just moving into new quarters, and not yet settled. I was discussing with a member of the faculty, the dean I think, about how many the room would hold, how soon it would be ready, and so on—just a business talk, nothing more—when he turned to me rather abruptly, looking me full in the face, and said with quiet deliberation: "I'm a member of church; I *think* I am a deacon in our church"—running his hand through his hair meditatively, as though to refresh his memory—"but I am not very much of a christian, sir." The smile that started to come to my face at the odd frankness of his remark was completely chased away by the distinct touch of pathos in both face and voice that seemed to speak of a hungry, unsatisfied heart within.

Perhaps it was a month or so later, in one of the mining towns down in the zinc belt of southwestern Missouri, I was to speak to a meeting of men. There were probably five or six hundred gathered in a Methodist Church. They were

strangers to me. I was in doubt what best to say
to them. One dislikes to fire ammunition at people
that are absent. So stepping down to a front pew
where several ministers were seated, I asked one
of them to run his eye over the house and tell me
what sort of a congregation it was, so far as he
knew them. He did so, and presently replied: "I
think fully two-thirds of these men are members
of our churches"—and then, with that same quizzical, half-laughing look, he added, "but you know,
sir, as well as I do, that not half of them are
christians worth counting." "Well," I said to myself, astonished, "this is a mining camp; this certainly is not anything like the condition of affairs
in the country generally."

But that series of incidents, coming one after
the other in such rapid succession, set me thinking
intently about that strange distinction between
being members of a church on the one hand, and
on the other, living lives that count and tell and
weigh for Jesus seven days in the week. I knew
that ministers had been recognizing such a distinction, but to find it so freely acknowledged by folks
in the pew was new, and surely significant.

And so I thought I would just ask the friends
here to-day very frankly, "What kind of Christians
are you?" I do not say what kind you are, for I
am a stranger, and do not know, and would only
think the best things of you. But I ask you frankly,
honestly now, as I ask myself anew, what kind are
you? Do you know? Because it makes such a
difference. The Master's plan—and what a genius
of a plan it is—is this, that the world should be
won, not by the preachers—though we must have

these men of God for teaching and leadership—but
by everyone who knows the story of Jesus *telling
someone*, and telling not only with his lips
earnestly and tactfully, but even more, *telling with
his life*. That is the Master's plan of campaign for
this world. And it makes a great difference to Him
and to the world outside whether you and I are
living the story of His love and power among men
or not.

Do you *know* what kind of a christian you are?
There are at least three others that do. First of all
there is Satan. He knows. Many of our church
officers are skilled in gathering and compiling
statistics, but they cannot hold a tallow-dip to
Satan in this matter of exact information. He is
the ablest of all statisticians, second only to one
other. He keeps careful record of every one of us,
and knows just how far we are interfering with
his plans. He knows that some of us—good, re-
spectable people, as common reckoning goes—
neither help God nor hinder Satan. Does that sound
rather hard? But is it not true? He has no objection to such people being counted in as christians.
Indeed, he rather prefers to have it so. Their
presence inside the church circle helps him mightily. *He* knows what kind of a christian you are.
Do *you* know?

Then there is the great outer circle of non-christian people—*they know*. Many of them are poorly
informed regarding the christian life; hungry for
something they have not, and know not just what
it is; with high ideals, though vague, of what a
christian life should be. And they look eagerly to
us for what they have thought we had, and are so

often keenly disappointed that our ideals, our life, is so much like others who profess nothing. And when here and there they meet one whose acts are dominated by a pure, high spirit, whose faces reflect a sweet radiance amid all circumstances, and whose lives send out a rare fragrance of gladness and kindliness and controlling peace, they are quick to recognize that, to them, intangible something that makes such people different. The world —tired, hungry, keen and critical for mere sham, appreciative of the real thing—the world knows what kind of christians we are. Do *we* know?

There is a third one watching us to-day with intense interest. The Lord Jesus! Sitting up yonder in glory, with the scar-marks of earth on face and form, looking eagerly down upon us who stand for Him in the world that crucified Him—*He knows.* I imagine Him saying, "There is that one down there whom I died for, who bears my name; *if* I had the *control* of that life what power I would gladly breathe in and out of it, but—he is *so absorbed in other things.*" The Master is thinking about you, studying your life, longing to carry out His plan if He could only get permission, and sorely disappointed in many of us. He knows. Do *you* know?

THE NIGHT VISITOR

After that trip I became much interested in discovering in John's Gospel some striking pictorial illustrations of these two kinds of christians, namely, those who have power in their lives for Jesus Christ and those who have not. Let me speak of only a few of these. The first is sketched briefly in the third chapter, with added touches in the seventh and nineteenth chapters. There is a little descriptive phrase used each time—"the man who came to Jesus by night." That comes to be in John's mind the most graphic and sure way of identifying this man. A good deal of criticism, chiefly among the upper classes, had already been aroused by Jesus' acts and words. This man Nicodemus clearly was deeply impressed by the young preacher from up in Galilee. He wants to find out more of him. But he shrank back from exposing himself to criticism by these influential people for his possible friendship with the young radical, as Jesus was regarded. So one day he waits until the friendly shadows will conceal his identity, and slipping quietly along the streets, close up to the houses so as to insure his purpose of not being recognized, he goes up yonder side street where Jesus has lodgings. He knocks timidly. "Does the preacher from up the north way stop here?" "Yes" "Could I see him?" He steps in and spends an evening in earnest conversation. I think we will all readily agree that Nicodemus *believed* Jesus after that night's interview, however he may have failed to understand all He said. Yes, we can say much more—he *loved* Him. For after the cruel crucifixion it is this man that brings a box of very precious spices, weighing as much as a hundred pounds, worth, without question, a large sum of money, with which to embalm the dead body of his friend. Ah! he loved Him. No one may question that.

But turn now to the seventh chapter of John. There is being held a special session of the Jewish

Senate in Jerusalem for the express purpose of
determining how to silence Jesus—to get rid of
Him. This man is a member of that body, and is
present. Yonder he sits with the others, listening
while his friend Jesus is being discussed and His
removal—by force if need be—is being plotted.
What does he do? What would you expect of a
friend of Jesus under such circumstances? I wonder what you and I would have done? I wonder
what we do do? Does he say modestly, but plainly,
"I spent a whole evening with this man, questioning Him, talking with Him, listening to Him. I feel
quite sure that He is our promised Messiah; and I
have decided to accept Him as such." Did he say
that? That would have been the simple truth. But
such a remark plainly would have aroused a storm
of criticism, and he dreaded that. Yet he felt that
something should be said. So, lawyer-like, he puts
the case abstractly. "Hmm—does our law judge
a man without giving him a fair hearing?" That
sounds fair, though it does seem rather feeble in
face of their determined opposition. But near by
sits a burly Pharisee, who turns sharply around
and, glaring savagely at Nicodemus, says sneer-
ingly: "Who are you? Do you come from Galilee,
too? Look and see! No prophet comes out of
Galilee"—with intensest contempt in the tone with
which he pronounces the word Galilee. And poor
Nicodemus seems to shrink back into half his
former size, and has not another word to say,
though all the facts, easily ascertainable, were
upon his side of the case. He loved Jesus without
doubt, but he had *no power* for Him among men
because of his timidity. Shall I use a plainer,

though uglier, word—his cowardice? That is not
a pleasant word to apply to a man. But is it not the
true word here? He was so afraid of what *they*
would think and say! Is that the sort of christian
you are? Believing Jesus, trusting Him, saved by
Him, loving Him, but shrinking back from speaking out for Him, tactfully, plainly, when opportunity presents or can be made. A christian, but
without positive power for Him among men
because of cowardice!

I can scarcely imagine Nicodemus walking down
the street in Jerusalem, arm in arm with another
Pharisee-member of the Sanhedrin and saying to
him quietly, but earnestly: "Have you had a talk
with this young man Jesus?" "No, indeed, I have
not!" "Well, do you know, I spent an evening
with Him down at His stopping place, and had a
long, careful talk with Him. I am quite satisfied
that He is our long-looked-for leader; I have decided to give Him my personal allegiance; won't
you get personally acquainted with Him? He is a
wonderful man." I say I have difficulty in thinking
that this man worked for Jesus like that. And yet
what more natural and proper, both for him and
for us? And what a difference it might have made
in many a man's life. *Powerless* for Jesus because
of timidity! Is that the kind *you* are? Possibly some
one thinks that rather hard on this man. Maybe
you are thinking of that other member of the
Sanhedrin—Joseph of Arimathea—who was also
a follower of Jesus, and that quite possibly he may
have been influenced by Nicodemus. Let us suppose, for Nicodemus' sake, that this is so, and then
mark the brief record of this man Joseph in John's

account: "A disciple *secretly* for *fear* of the Jews."
If we may fairly presume that it was Nicodemus'
influence that led his friend Joseph to follow Jesus,
yet he had led him no nearer than he himself had
gone! He *could* lead him no higher or nearer than
that.

John in his gospel makes plain the fact that
Jesus suffered much from these secret, timid, cowardly disciples whose fear of men gripped them as
in a vise. Five times he makes special mention of
these people who believed Jesus, but cravenly
feared to line up with Him.[1] He even says that
many of the *rulers*—the very class that plotted
and voted His death—believed Jesus, but that *fear*
of *the others* shut their lips and drove them into
the shadow when they could have helped Him
most. These people seem to have left numerous
descendants, many of whom continue with us unto
this day.

TIGHTLY TIED UP

Turn now to the eleventh chapter and you will
find another pictorial suggestion of this same sort
of *powerless christian,* though in this instance
made so by another reason. It is the Bethany
Chapter, the Lazarus Chapter. The scene is just
out of Bethany village. There is a man lying dead
in the cave yonder. Here stands Jesus. There are
the disciples, and Martha, and Mary, and the
villagers, and a crowd from Jerusalem. The Master
is speaking. His voice rings out clear and com-
manding—"Lazarus, come forth"—speaking to a

[1] John 3:1. 7:50. 12:42 with 9:22. 19:38, 39.

dead man. And the simple record runs, "He that
was dead"—life comes between those two lines of
the record—"came forth, bound hand and foot
with grave-clothes, and his face was bound about
with a napkin." Will you please take a look at
Lazarus as he steps from the tomb? Do you think
his eyes are dull, or his cheeks hollow and pale?
I think not! When Jesus, the Lord of life, gives
life, either physical or spiritual, He gives abundant
life. That face may have been a bit spare. There
had been no food for at least four days and likely
longer. But there is the flash of health in his eye
and the ruddy hue of good blood in his cheek. He
has life. But look closer. He is bound hand and
foot and face. He can neither walk nor work nor
speak.

I have met some christian people who reminded
me forcibly of that scene. They are christians.
The Master has spoken life, and they have re-
sponded to His word. But they are so tied up with
the grave-clothes of the old life that there can be
none of the power of free action in life or service.
May I ask you very kindly, but very plainly, are
you like that? Is that the reason you have so little
power with God, and for God? Perhaps some one
would say, "Just what do you mean?" I mean this:
that there may be some personal habit of yours, or
perhaps some society custom which you practice,
or it may be some business method, or possibly an
old friendship which you have carried over into
the new life from the old that is seriously hindering your christian life. It may be something that
goes into your mouth or comes out of it that prevents those lips speaking for the Master. Perhaps

it is some organization you belong to. If there is lack of freedom and power for Christ you may be sure there is *something* that is blighting your life and dwarfing your usefulness. It may possibly be that practically in your daily life you are exerting no more power for God than a dead man! A christian, indeed, but *without power because of compromise* with something questionable or outrightly wrong! Is that so with you? I do not say it is, for I do not know. But *you* know. The hungry, critical world knows. Subtle, keen Satan knows. The Lord Jesus knows. Do you know if that describes you? You may know with certainty within twenty-four hours if you wish to and will to. May we be willing to have the Spirit's searchlight turned in upon us tonight.

THE MASTER'S IDEAL

There is another kind of christian, an utterly different kind, spoken of and illustrated in this same Gospel of John, and I doubt not many of them also are here. It is *Jesus' ideal* of what a christian should be. Have you sometimes wished you could have a few minutes of quiet talk with Jesus? I mean face to face, as two of us might sit and talk together. You have thought you would ask Him to say very simply and plainly just what He expects of you. Well, I believe He would answer in words something like those of this seventh chapter of John. It was at the time of Feast of Tabernacles. There was a vast multitude of Jews there from all parts of the world. It was like an immense convention, but larger than any convention we know. The

people were not entertained in the homes, but lived
for seven days in leafy booths made of branches of
trees. It was the last day of the feast. There was a
large concourse of people gathered in one of the
temple areas; not women, but men; not sitting, but
standing. Up yonder stand the priests, pouring
water out of large jars, to symbolize the outpouring
of the Holy Spirit upon the nation of Israel. Just
then Jesus speaks, and amid the silence of the
intently watching throng His voice rings out: "If
any man thirst let him come unto Me and drink;
he that believeth on Me, as the Scripture saith,
out of his belly shall flow rivers of living water."
Mark that significant closing clause. That packs
into a sentence Jesus' ideal of what a true christian
down in this world should be, and may be. Every
word is full of meaning.

The heart of the sentence is in the last word—
"water." *Water* is an essential of life. Absence
of water means suffering and sickness, dearth and
death. Plenty of good water means *life*. All the
history of the world clusters about the water
courses. Study the history of the rivers, the sea-
shores, and lake edges, and you know the history
of the earth. Those men who heard Jesus speak
would instinctively think of the Jordan. It was their
river. Travelers say that no valley exceeded in
beauty and fruitfulness that valley of the Jordan,
made so by those swift waters. No hillside so fair
in their green beauty, nor so wealthy in heavy loads
of fruit as those sloping down to the edge of that
stream. Now plainly Jesus is talking of something
that may, through us, exert as decided an influence
upon the lives of those we touch as water has

exerted, and still exerts, on the history of the earth, and as this Jordan did in that wonderful, historic Palestine. Mark the quantity of water— "rivers." Not a Jordan merely, that would be wonderful enough, but Jordans—a Jordan, and a Nile, and a Euphrates, a Yang Tse Kiang, and an Olga and a Rhine, a Seine and a Thames, and a Hudson and an Ohio—"*rivers*." Notice, too, the *kind* of water. Like this racing, turbulent, muddy Jordan? No, no! "rivers of *living* water," "water of *life*, clear as crystal." You remember in Ezekiel's vision which we read together that the waters constantly increased in depth, and that everywhere they went there was healing, and abundant life, and prosperity, and beauty, and food, and a continual harvest the year round, and all because of the waters of the river. They were veritable waters of life.

Now mark that little, but very significant, phrase —"*Out of*"—not *into,* but "out of." All the difference in the lives of men lies in the difference between these two expressions. "Into" is the world's preposition. Every stream turns in; and that means *a dead sea.* Many a man's life is simply the coast line of a dead sea. "Out of" is the Master's word. His thought is of others. The stream must flow in, and must flow through if it is to flow out, but it is judged by its direction, and Jesus would turn it outward. There must be good connections upward, and a clear channel inward, but the objective point is outward toward a parched earth. But before it can flow out it must *fill up.* An *out*flow in this case means an *over*flow. There must be a flooding inside before there can be a flowing out. And let the fact be carefully marked that it is only

the overflow from the fullness within our own
lives that brings refreshing to anyone else. A man
praying at a conference in England for the outpouring of the Holy Spirit said: "O, Lord, we can't
hold much, but we can overflow lots." That is
exactly the Master's thought. "Out of his belly
shall flow rivers of living water."

Do you remember that phrase in the third chapter of Joshua—"For Jordan overfloweth all its
banks all the time of harvest." When there was a
flood in the river, there was a harvest in the land.
Has there been a harvest in your life? A harvest of
the fruit of the spirit—love, joy, peace, long-suffering; a harvest of souls? "No," do you say, "not
much of a harvest, I am afraid," or it may be your
heart says "none at all." Is it hard to tell why? Has
there been a flood-tide in your heart, a filling up
from above until the blessed stream had to find an
outlet somewhere, and produce a harvest? A harvest outside means a rising of the tide inside. A
flooding of the heart always brings a harvest in the
life. A few years ago there were great floods in the
southern states, and the cotton and corn crops
following were unprecedented. Paul reminded his
Roman friends that when the Holy Spirit has free
swing in the life "the love of God *floods* our
hearts." [1]

Please notice, too, the *source* of the stream—
"out of his belly." Will you observe for a moment
the rhetorical figure here? I used to suppose it
meant "out of his *heart*." The ancients, you remember, thought the heart lay down in the ab-
dominal region. But you will find that this book

[1] Rom. 5:5.

is very exact in its use of words. The blood is the
life. The heart pumps the blood, but the stomach
makes it. The seat of life is not in the heart, but
in the stomach. If you will take down a book of
physiology, and find the chart showing the circula-
tion of the blood, you will see a wonderful network
of lines spreading out in every direction, but all
running, through lighter lines into heavier, and
still blacker, until every line converges in the great
stomach artery. *And everywhere the blood goes
there is life.* Now turn to a book of physical
geography and get a map showing the water system of some great valley like the Mississippi, and
you will find a striking reproduction of the other
chart. And if you will shut your eyes and imagine
the reality back of that chart, you will see hundreds
of cool, clear springs flowing successively into runs,
brooks, creeks, larger streams, river branches,
rivers, and finally into the great river—the reservoir of all. *And everywhere the waters go there is
life.* The only difference between these two streams
of life is in the direction. The blood flows from the
largest toward the smallest; the water flows from
the smallest toward the largest. Both bring life
with its accompaniments of beauty and vigor and
fruitfulness. There is Jesus' picture of the Christian
down in the world. As the red stream flows out
from the stomach, and, propelled by the force-
pump of the heart, through a marvelous network
of minute rivers takes life to every part of the
body, so "he that believeth on Me"—that is the vital
connecting link with the great origin of this stream
of life—out of the very source of life within him
shall go *a flood-tide of life,* bringing refreshing,

and cleansing, and beauty, and vigor everywhere within the circle of his life, even though, like the red streams and the water streams, he be unconscious of it.

AN UNLIKELY CHANNEL

What a marvelous conception of the power of life! How strikingly it describes Jesus' own earthly life! But there is something more marvelous still— He means that ideal to become real in you, my friend, and in me. I doubt not there are some here whose eager hearts are hungry for just such a life, but who art tremblingly conscious of their own weakness. Your thoughts are saying: "I wish I *could* live such a life, but certainly this is not for *me;* this man talking doesn't know *me*—no special talent or opportunity: such strong tides of temptation that sweep me clean off my feet—not for me." Ah, my friend, I verily believe you are the very one the Master had in mind, for He had John put into his gospel a living illustration of this ideal of His that goes down to the very edge of human unlikeliness and inability. He goes down to the lowest so as to include all. What proved true in this case may prove true with you, and much more. The story is in the fourth chapter. It is a sort of advance page of the Book of Acts. A sample of the power of Pentecost before the day of Pentecost. You and I live on the flood-side of Pentecost. This illustration belongs back where the streams had only just commenced trickling. It is a miniature. You and I may furnish the life-size if we will.

It is the story of a woman; not a man, but a

woman. One of the *weaker* sex, so called. She was ignorant, prejudiced, and without social standing. She was a woman of no reputation. Aye, worse than that, of bad reputation. She probably had less moral influence in her town than any one here has in his circle. Could a more unlikely person have been used? But she came in touch with the Lord Jesus. She yielded herself to that touch. There lies the secret of what follows. That contact radically changed her. She went back to her village and commenced speaking about Jesus to those she knew. She could not preach; she simply told plainly and earnestly what she knew and believed about Him. And the result is startling. There are hundreds of ministers who are earnestly longing for what came so easily to her. What modern people call a revival began at once. We are told in the simple language of the Gospel record that *"many believed on Him because of the word of the woman."* They had not seen Jesus yet. He was up by the well. They were down in the village. She was an ignorant woman, of formerly sinful life. But there is the record of the wonderful result of her simple witnessing—they believed on Jesus because of the word of that woman. There is only one way to account for such results. Only the Holy Spirit speaking through her lips could have produced them. She had commenced drinking of the living water of which Jesus had been talking to her, and now already the rivers were flowing out to others.

What Jesus did with her, He longs to do with you, *and far more,* if you will let Him; though his plan for using you may be utterly different from the one He had for her, and so the particular results different. Now let me ask very frankly why have we not all such power for our Master as she? The Master's plan is plain. He said "ye shall have power." But so many of us do not have! Why not? Well, possibly some of us are like Nicodemus— there is no power because of timidity, cowardice, fear of what *they* will think, or say. Possibly some of us are in the same condition spiritually that Lazarus was in physically. We are tied up tight, hands and feet and face. Some sin, some compromise, some hushing of that inner voice, *something* wrong. Some little thing, you may say. Humph! as though anything *could* be little that is wrong! *Sin is never little!*

A Clogged Channel

Out in Colorado they tell of a little town nestled down at the foot of some hills—a sleepy-hollow village. You remember the rainfall is very slight out there, and they depend much upon irrigation. But some enterprising citizens ran a pipe up the hills to a lake of clear, sweet water. As a result the town enjoyed a bountiful supply of water the year round without being dependent upon the doubtful rainfall. And the population increased and the place had quite a western boom. One morning the housewives turned the water spigots, but no water came. There was some sputtering. There is apt to be noise when there is nothing else. The men climbed the hill. There was the lake full as ever. They examined around the pipes as well as possible, but could find no break. Try as they might, they could find no cause for the stoppage. And as days grew into weeks, people commenced moving away again, the grass grew in the streets, and the prosperous town was going back to its old sleepy condition when one day one of the town officials received a note. It was poorly written, with bad spelling and grammar, but he never cared less about writing or grammar than just then. It said in effect: "Ef you'll jes pull the plug out of the pipe about eight inches from the top you'll get all the water you want." Up they started for the top of the hill, and examining the pipe, found the plug which some vicious tramp had inserted. Not a very big plug—just big enough to fill the pipe. It is surprising how large a reservoir of water can be held back by how small a plug. Out came the plug; down came the water freely; by and by back came prosperity again.

Why is there such a lack of power in our lives? The reservoir up yonder is full to overflowing, with clear, sweet, life-giving water. And here all around us the earth is so dry, so thirsty, cracked open— huge cracks like dumb mouths asking mutely for what we should give. And the connecting pipes between the reservoir above and the parched plain below are there. Why then do not the refreshing waters come rushing down? The answer is very plain. You know why. *There is a plug in the pipe.* Something in us clogging up the channel and nothing can get through. How shall we have power, abundant, life-giving, sweetening our own lives, and changing those we touch? The answer

is easy for me to give—it will be much harder for
us all to do—*pull out the plug*. Get out the thing
that you know is hindering.

I am going to ask every one who will, to offer
this simple prayer—and I am sure every thoughtful, earnest man and woman here will. Just bow
your head and quietly under your breath say to
Him, "Lord Jesus, show me what there is in my
life that is displeasing to Thee; what there is Thou
wouldst change." You may be sure He will. He is
faithful. He will put His finger on that tender spot
very surely. Then add a second clause to that
prayer—"By Thy grace helping me, *I will put it out*
whatever it may cost, or wherever it may cut."
Shall we bow our heads and offer that prayer, and
hew close to that line, steadily, faithfully? It will
open up a life of marvelous blessing undreamed
of for you and everyone you touch.

The Olivet
Message

SEARCHLIGHT SIGHTS

Coming into Cleveland harbor one evening, just
after nightfall, a number of passengers were gathered on the upper deck eagerly watching the
colored breakwater lights and the city lights beyond. Suddenly a general curiosity was aroused
by a small boat of some sort, on the left, scudding
swiftly along in the darkness like a blacker streak
on the black waters. A few of us who chanced to
be near the captain on the smaller deck above,
heard him quietly say, "Turn on the searchlight."
Almost instantly an intense white light shone full
on the stranger-boat, bringing it to view so distinctly that we could almost count the nail-heads,
and the strands in her cordage.

If some of us here to-night have made the prayer
suggested in our last talk together—Lord Jesus,
show me what there is in my life that is displeasing
to Thee, that Thou wouldst change—we will ap-

preciate something of the power of that Lake Erie
searchlight. There is a searchlight whiter, intenser,
more keenly piercing than any other. Into every
heart that desires, and will hold steadily open to it,
the Lord Jesus will turn that searching light. Then
you will begin to see things *as they actually are.*
And that sight may well lead to discouragement.
Many a hidden thing, which you are glad enough
to have hidden, will be plainly seen. How is it possible, you will be ready to ask, for me to lead the
life the Master's ambition has planned for me,
with such mixed motives, selfish ambitions, sinfulness and weakness as I am beginning to get a
glimpse of—how is it possible?

There is one answer to that intense heart-ques-
tion, and only one. *We must have power,* some
supernatural power, something outside of us, and
above us, and far greater than we, to come in and
win the victory within us and for us.

If that young man whose inner life is passion-
swept, one tidal wave of fierce temptation, hot on
the heels of the last, until all the moorings are
snapped, and he driven rudderless out to sea—if
he is to ride masterfully upon that sea *he must
have power.*

If that young woman is to be as attractive, and
womanly winsome in the society circle where she
moves, as she is meant to be, and yet able to shape
her lips into a gently uttered, but rock-ribbed *no*
when certain well-understood questionable matters
come up, *she must have power.* If society young
people are to remain in the world, and yet not be
swayed by its spirit: on one side not prudish, nor
fanatical, nor extreme, but cheery, and radiant,

and full-lived, and yet free of those compromising entanglements that are common to society everywhere, *they must have a rare pervasive power.*

For that business man down in the sharp competition of the world where duty calls him, to resist the sly temptations to overreach, to keep keenly alert not to be overreached; and through all to preserve an uncensorious spirit, unhurt by the selfishness of the crowd—tell me, some of you men— *will that not take power?* Aye, more power than some of us know about, yet.

For that same man to go through his store and remove from shelf or counter some article which yields a good profit, but which he knows his Master would not have there—Ah! *that'll take power.*

It takes power to keep the body under control: the mouth clean and sweet, both physically and morally: the eye turned away from the thing that should not be thought about: the ear closed to what should not enter that in-gate of the heart: to allow no picture to hang upon the walls of your imagination that may not hang upon the walls of your home: to keep every organ of the body pure for nature's holy function only—*that takes mighty power.*

For that young man to be wide-awake, a pusher in business, and yet steadily, determinedly to hold back any crowding of the other side of his life: the inner side, the outer-helpful side, the Bible-reading- and secret-prayer- and quiet personal-work-side of his life, *that will take real power.*

It will take a power that some of us have not known to let that glass go untouched, and that quieting drug untasted and unhandled. If the rear end of some pharmacies could speak out, many a story would startle our ears of struggles and defeats that tell sadly of utter lack of power.

It takes power for the man of God in the pulpit to speak plainly about particular sins before the faces of those who are living in them; and *still more power* to do it with the rare tactfulness and tenderness of the Galilean preacher. *It takes power* to stick to the Gospel story and the old book, when literature and philosophy present such fine opportunities for the essays that are so enjoyable and that bring such flattering notice. *It takes power* to leave out the finely woven rhetoric that you are disposed to put in for the sake of the compliment it will bring from that literary woman down yonder, or that bright, brainy young lawyer in the fifth pew on the left aisle. *It takes power* to see that the lips that speak for God are thoroughly clean lips, and the life that stands before that audience a pure life.

It takes power to keep sweet in the home, where if anywhere, the seamy side is apt to stick out. How many wooden oaths could kicked chairs and slammed doors tell of! After all the home-life comes close to being the real test of power, does it not? *It takes power* to be gracious and strong, and patient and tender, and cheery, in the commonplace things, and the commonplace places, does it not?

Now, I have something to tell you to-night that to me is very wonderful, and constantly growing in wonder. It is this—*the Master has thought of all that!* He has thought into your life. Yes, I mean *your particular life,* and made an arrangement to fully cover all your need of power. He stands anew in our midst to-day, and putting His pierced hand gently upon your arm, His low, loving, clear voice says quietly, but very distinctly, *"You—you shall have power."* For every subtle, strong temptation, for every cry of need, for every low moan of disappointment, for every locking of the jaws in the resolution of despair, for every disheartened look out into the morrow, for every yearningly ambitious heart there comes to-night that unmistakable ringing promise of His—*ye shall have power.*

THE OLIVET MESSAGE

Our needs argue the necessity of power. And the argument is strengthened by the peculiar emphasis of the Master's words. Do you remember that wondrous Olivet scene? In the quiet twilight of a Sabbath evening a group of twelve young men stand yonder on the brow of Olives. The last glowing gleams of the setting sun fill all the western sky, and shed a halo of yellow glory-light over the hilltop, through the trees, in upon that group. You instantly pick out the leader. No mistaking Him. And around Him group the eleven men who have lived with Him these months past, now eagerly gazing into that marvelous face, listening for His words. He is going away. They know that. Coming back soon, they understand. But in His absence the work He has begun is to be entrusted to their hands. And so with ears and eyes they listen intently for the good-bye word—His last message. It will mean so much in the coming days.

Two things the Master says. The first is that

ringing "go ye" so familiar to every true heart. The second is a very decisive, distinct *"but tarry ye."* What, wait still longer! Tarry, now, when your great work is done! Listen again, while His parting words cut the air with their startling distinctness *"but tarry ye—until ye be endued with power."*

I could readily imagine impulsive Peter quickly saying, "What! shall we *tarry* when the whole world is dying! Do we not *know* enough now?" And the Master's answer would come in that clear, quiet voice of His, "yes, tarry: you have knowledge enough but *knowledge is not enough,* there must be power."

There is knowledge enough within the christian church of every land—aye, knowledge enough within the walls of this building to-night to convert the world, if knowledge would do it. Into many a life, through home training, and school, and college, has come knowledge, while power lingers without—a stranger. Knowledge—the twin idol with gold to American hearts—is essential, but let it be plainly said, is not *the* essential. Knowledge is the fuel piled up in the fireplace. The mantel is of carved oak, and the fenders so highly polished they seem almost to send out warmth, but the thermometer is working down toward zero, and the people are shivering. The spark of living fire is essential. Then how all changes! There must be fire from above to kindle our knowledge and ourselves before any of the needed results will come.

There is no language strong enough to tell how absolutely needful it is that every follower of Jesus Christ from the one most prominent in leadership down to the very humblest disciple, shall receive this promised power.

Look at these men Jesus is talking to. There is Peter, the man of rock, and John and James, the sons of thunder. They were with the Lord on the Transfiguration Mount, and when He raised the dead. They were near by during the awful agony of Gethsemane. They were admitted nearer to the Master's inner life than any others. There is quiet matter-of-fact Andrew, who had a reputation for bringing others to Jesus. There is Nathanael, in whom is no guile. It is to these men that there comes that positive command to tarry. If *they* needed such a command, do not we?

"Yes," someone says, "I understand that this power you speak of is something the leaders and preachers must have, but you scarcely mean that there is the same necessity for us people down in the ranks, and that we are to expect the same power as these others, do you?" Will you please call to mind that original Pentecost company? There were one hundred and twenty of them. And while there was a Peter being prepared to preach that tremendous sermon, and a John to write five books of the New Testament and probably a James to preside over the affairs of the Jerusalem Church, and possibly a Stephen, and a Philip, yet these are only a few. By far the greater number, both men and women, are unnamed and unknown. Just the common, every-day folk, the filling-in of society; aye, the very foundation of all society. They had no prominent part to play. But they accepted the Master's promise of power, and His command to

wait, *as made to them.* And as a result *they, too,*
were filled with the Holy Spirit, that wonderful
morning. I think, very likely, "the good man of the
house" whose guest Jesus was that last night was
there, and all the Marys, including the Bethany
Mary, who simply sat at His feet, and the Magda-
lene Mary, and housekeeper Martha, and maybe
that little lad whose loaves and fishes had been
used about a year before. That was the sort of company that prayerfully, with one accord, not only
waited but *received* that never-to-be-forgotten filling of the Holy Spirit.

Certainly, as some of you think, the preacher
must have this promised power peculiarly for his
leadership. But just as really he needs it *because he
is a man for his living,* to make him sweet and
gentle and patient down in his home: to make him
sympathetic and strong in his constant contact with
the hungry hearts he must meet. That young me-
chanic must have this promised power if he is to
live an earnest, manly life in that shop. That school
girl, whose home duties crowd her time so; that
keen-minded student working for honors amid
strong competition; these society young people;
these all need, above all else, this promised power
that in, and through, and around and above all of
their lives may be a wholesomely sweet, earnest
Christliness, pervading the life even as the odor of
flowers pervades a room.

Do you remember Paul's list of the traits of character that mark a christian life—love, joy, peace,
long-suffering, gentleness, goodness, meekness,
faithfulness, self-control? [1] Suppose for a moment

[1] Gal. 5:22.

you think through a list of the opposites of those
nine characteristics—bitterness, envy, hate, low-
spiritedness, sulkiness, chafing, fretting, worrying,
short-suffering, quick-temper, hot-temper, high-
spiritedness, unsteadiness, unreliability, lack of
control of yourself. May I ask, have you any personal acquaintance with some of these qualities?
Is there still some need in your life for the other
desirable traits? Well, remember that it is only as
the Holy Spirit has *control* that this fruit of His is
found. For notice that it is not we that bear this
fruit, but He in us. We furnish the soil. He must
have free swing in its cultivation if He is to get
this harvest. And notice, too, that it does not say
"the *fruits* of the Spirit," as though *you* might have
one or more, and *I* have some others. But it is
"fruit"—that is, it is all one fruit and all of it is
meant to be growing up in each one of us. And let
the fact be put down as settled once for all that
only as we tarry and receive the Master's promise
of power can we live the lives He longs to have us
live down here among men for Him.

If that father is so to live at home before those
wide-awake, growing boys that he can keep up the
family altar, and instead of letting it become a
mere irksome form, make it the green, fresh spot
in the home life, he must have this promised power,
for he cannot do it of himself. I presume *some* of
you fathers know that.

There is that mother, living in what would be
reckoned a humble home, one of a thousand like
it, but charged with the most sacred trust ever
committed to human hands—*the molding of precious lives*. If there be hallowed ground anywhere

surely it is there in the life of that home. What patience and tirelessness, and love and tact and wisdom and wealth of resource does that woman not need! Ah, mothers! if any one needs to tarry and receive the power promised by the Son of that Mary, who was filled with the Holy Spirit from before His birth for her sacred trust, *surely you do*.

Here sits one whose life plans seem to have gone all askew. The thing you love to do, and had fondly planned over, removed utterly beyond your reach, and you compelled to fit in to something for which you have no taste. It will take nothing less than the power the Master promised for you to go on faithfully, cheerfully just where you have been placed, no repining, no complaining, even in your innermost soul, but, instead, a glad, joyous fitting into the Father's plan with a radiant light in the face. Only His power can accomplish that victory! But *His can*. And His may be yours for the tarrying and the taking.

Let me repeat then with all the emphasis possible that as certainly as you need to trust Jesus Christ for your soul's salvation, you also need to receive this power of the Holy Spirit to work that salvation out *in your present life*.

A DOUBLE CENTER

It has helped me greatly in understanding the Master's insistent emphasis upon the promise of power to keep clearly in mind that the christian system of truth revolves around a double center. It is illustrated best not by a circle with its single center, but by an ellipse with its twin centers.

There are two central truths—not one, but two.
The first of the two is grained deep down in the
common Christian teaching and understanding. If
I should ask any group of Sabbath school children
in this town, next Sabbath morning, the question:
What is the most important thing we christians
believe? Amid the great variety in the form of
answer would come, in substance, without doubt,
this reply: *"The blood of Jesus Christ cleanseth
from all sin."* And they would be right. But there is
a second truth—very reverently and thoughtfully
let me say—of *equal importance* with that; namely,
this: *the Holy Spirit empowereth against all sin,
and for life and service.* These two truths are co-
ordinate. They run in parallel lines. They belong
together. They are really two halves of the one
great truth. But this second half needs emphasis,
because it has not always been put into its proper
place beside the other.

Jesus died on the cross to make freedom from
sin *possible.* The Holy Spirit dwells within me to
make freedom from sin *actual.* The Holy Spirit
does *in* me what Jesus did *for* me. The Lord Jesus
makes a deposit in the bank on my account. The
Spirit checks the money out and puts it into my
hands. Jesus does in me now by His Spirit what He
did for me centuries ago on the cross, in His person.

Now these two truths, or two parts of the same
truth, go together in God's plan, but, with some
exceptions, have not gone together in men's experience. That explains why so many christian lives
are a failure and a reproach. The Church of Christ
has been gazing so intently upon the hill of the
cross with its blood-red message of sin and love,

that it has largely lost sight of the Ascension Mount
with its legacy of power. We have been so enwrapt
with that marvelous scene on Calvary—and what
wonder!—that we have allowed ourselves to lose
the intense significance of Pentecost. That last victorious shout—"It is finished"—has been crowding out in our ears its counterpart—the equally
victorious cry of Olivet—*"All power hath been
given unto Me."*

The christian's range of vision must always take
in two hill-tops—Calvary and Olivet. Calvary—
sin conquered through the blood of Jesus, a matter
of history. Olivet—sin conquered through the
power of Jesus, a matter of experience. When the
subject is spoken of, we are apt to say: "Yes, that
is correct, I understand that." But *do* we understand it in our *experience*? So certainly as I must
trust Jesus as my Saviour so certainly must I constantly yield my life to the control of the Spirit of
Jesus if I am to find real the practical power of His
salvation.

As surely as men are now urged to accept Jesus
as the great step in life, so surely should they be
instructed to yield themselves to the Holy Spirit's
control that Jesus' plan for their lives may be
carried through.

You remember in the olden time the Hebrew
men were required to appear before God in the
appointed place three times during the year. At the
Passover, and at Pentecost, and again at the harvest home feast of Tabernacles. So it is required
of every man of us who would fit his life into God's
plan that he shall first of all come to the Passover
feast, where Christ our Passover is sacrificed for us.

And then that he shall as certainly come to the great Pentecost feast, or feast of first fruits where a glorified Passover Lamb breathes down His Spirit of power into the life. And then he is sure to have a constant attendance at a first-fruits feast all his days, with a great harvest home festival at the end.

I said there were two central truths. Will you notice that the gospels put it also in this way, that *Jesus came to do two things*—not one thing, but *two* things—in working out our salvation. That the first is dependent for its practical power upon the second, and the second is the completing or carrying into effect of the power of the first. That the first—let me say it with great reverence—is valueless without the second.

What *was* Jesus' mission? Would you not expect His forerunner to understand it? Listen, then, to his words. When questioned specifically by the official deputation sent from the national leaders at Jerusalem, he pointed to Jesus, and declared that He had come for a two-fold purpose. Listen: "Behold the Lamb of God who beareth away the sin of the world"; and then he added, and the word comes to us with the peculiar emphasis of repetition by each of the four gospel scribes—"this is He that baptizeth with the Holy Spirit." That was spoken to them originally without doubt in a national sense. It just as surely applies to every one of us in a personal sense.

Mark also the emphasis of *Jesus' own teachings* regarding this second part of His mission. At the very beginning He spoke the decided words about the necessity of being born of the Spirit. And we are all impressed with that fact. But observe that several times, in the brief gospel record, He refers the disciples to the overshadowing importance of the *Spirit's control in the life*. And that He devotes a large part of that last long confidential talk which John records, to this special subject, pointing out the new experiences to come with the coming of the Spirit, and holding out to them as the greatest evidence of His own love *the promise of power*.

It adds intense emphasis to all this to note that Jesus Himself, very Son of God, was in that wonderful human life of His utterly dependent upon the Holy Spirit. At the very outset, before venturing upon a single act or word of His appointed ministry, He waits at the Jordan waters, until the promised anointing of power came. What a picture does that prayerfully waiting Jesus present to powerless men to-day! From that moment every bit and part of His life was under the control of that Holy Spirit. Impelled into the wilderness for that fierce set-to with Satan, coming back to Galilee within the power of the Spirit, He himself clearly stated more than once, that it was through this anointing that He preached, and taught, and healed, and cast out demons. The writer of the Hebrews assures us that it was through the power of the Eternal Spirit that He was enabled to go through the awful experiences of Gethsemane and Calvary. And Luke adds that it was through the same empowering Spirit that He gave commandment to the apostles for the stupendous task of world-wide evangelization.. And then at the very last referring them to that life of His, He said: "As the father hath sent Me even so send I you." Let me ask if He, very God of very God, yet in His earthly life intensely human, needed that anointing, do not we? If He waited for that experience before venturing upon any service, shall not you and I?

But we must turn to the book of Acts to get fully within the grip of this truth. For it, with the epistles fitting into it, is peculiarly the *Holy Spirit book*, even as the Old Testament is the *Jehovah book* and the gospels with Revelation the *Jesus book*. The climax of the gospels is in the Acts. What is promised in the gospels is *experienced* in the Acts.

Jesus is dominant in the gospels; the Spirit of Jesus in the Acts. He is the only continuous personality from first to last. He is the common denominator of the book. The first twelve chapters group about Peter, the remaining sixteen about Paul, but distinctly above both they all group about the Holy Spirit. He is the one dominant factor throughout. The first fourth of the book is fairly aflame with His presence at the center—Jerusalem. Thence out to Samaria, and through the Cornelius door to the whole outer non-Jewish world; at Antioch the new center, and thence through the uttermost parts of the Roman empire into its heart, His is the presence recognized and obeyed. He is ceaselessly guiding, empowering, inspiring, checking, controlling clear to the abrupt end. His is the one mastering personality. And everywhere His presence is a transforming presence. Nothing short of startling is the change in Peter, in the attitude of the Jerusalem thousands, in the persecutor Saul, in the spirit of these disciples, in the unprecedented and unparalleled unselfishness shown. It is revolu-

tionary. Ah! it was meant to be so. This book is the
living illustration of what Jesus meant by His
teaching regarding His successor. It becomes also
an acted illustration of what the personal christian
life is meant to be.

The Spirit's presence and the necessity of His
control is deep-grained in the consciousness of the
leaders in this book. Leaving the stirring scenes at
the capital the eighth chapter takes us down to
Samaria. Multitudes have been led to believe
through the preaching of a man who has been
chosen to look after the business matters of the
church. Peter and John are sent down to aid the
new movement. Note that their very first concern
is to spend time in prayer that this great company
may receive the Holy Spirit.

The next chapter shifts the scene to Damascus.
A man unknown save for this incident is sent as
God's messenger to Saul. As he lays his hand upon
this chosen man and speaks the light-giving words
he instinctively adds, "and be filled with the Holy
Spirit." That is not recorded as a part of what he
had been told to do. But plainly this humble man
of God believes that that is the essential element in
Saul's preparation for his great work.

In the tenth chapter the Holy Spirit's action with
Cornelius completely upsets the life-long, rock-
rooted ideas of these intensely national, and intensely exclusive Jews. Yet it is accepted as final.

With what quaint simplicity does the thirteenth
chapter tell of the Holy Spirit's initiation of those
great missionary journeys of Paul from the new
center of world evangelization? "the Holy Spirit
said, etc." And how like it is the language of
James in delivering the judgment of the first

church council:—"it seemed good to the Holy Spirit and to us."

Paul's conviction is very plain from numerous references in those wonderful heart-searching and heart-revealing letters of his. But one instance in this Book of Acts will serve as a fair illustration of his teaching and habit. It is in the nineteenth chapter. In his travels he has come as far as to Ephesus, and finds there a small company of earnest disciples. They are strangers to him. He longs to help them, but must first find their need. At once he puts a question to them. A question may be a great revealer. This one reveals his own conception of what must be the pivotal experience of every true follower of Jesus. He asks: "Did ye receive the Holy Spirit when ye believed?"

But they had been poorly instructed, like many others since, and were not clear just what he meant. They had received the baptism of John— a baptism of repentance; but not the baptism of Jesus—a baptism of power. And Paul at once gives himself up to instructing and then praying with them until the promised gift is graciously bestowed. That is the last we hear of those twelve persons. Some of them may have been women. Some may have come to be leaders in that great Ephesian Church. But of that nothing is said. The emphasis remains on the fact that in Paul's mind because they were followers of the Lord Jesus they must have this empowering experience of the Holy Spirit's infilling.

Plainly in this Book of Acts the pivot on which all else rests and turns is the unhindered presence of the Holy Spirit.

Five Essentials

If you will stop a while to think into it you will find that a rightly rounded christian life has five essential characteristics. I mean essential in the same sense as that light is an essential to the eye. The eye's seeing depends wholly on light. If it does not see light, by and by it cannot see light. The ear that hears no sound loses the power to hear sound. Light is essential to the healthful eye: sound to the ear: air to the lungs: blood to the heart. Just as really are these five things essential to a strong healthful christian life.

The *second* of these is a heart-love for the old Book of God. Not reading it as a duty—taking a chapter at night because you feel you must. I do not mean that just now. But reading it because you *love* to; as you would a love letter or a letter from home. Thinking about it as the writer of the one hundred and nineteenth psalm did. Listen to him for a moment in that one psalm, talking about this book: "I delight," "I will delight," "My delight"—in all nine times. "I love," "Oh! how I love," "I do love," "Consider how I love," "I love exceedingly," again nine times in all. "I have longed," "My eyes fail," "My soul breaketh," speaking of the intensity of his desire to get alone with the book. "Sweeter than honey," "As great spoil," "As much as all riches," "Better than thousands of gold," "Above gold, yea, above fine gold." And all that packed into less than two leaves. Do you love this Book like that? Would you like to? Wait a moment.

The *third* essential is right habits of prayer. Living a veritable life of prayer. Making prayer the chief part not alone of your life, but of your service. Having answers to prayer as a constant experience. Being like the young man in a conference in India, who said, "I used to pray three times a day: Now I pray only once a day, and that is *all* day." Feet busy all the day, hands ceaselessly active, head full of matters of business, but the heart never out of communication with Him. Has prayer never become to you like that? Would you have it so? Wait a moment.

The *fourth* essential is a pure, earnest, unselfish life. Our lives are the strongest part of us—or else the weakest. A man knows the least of the influence of his own life. Life is not mere length of time but the daily web of character we unconsciously weave. Our thoughts, imaginations, purposes, motives, love, will, are the under threads: our words, tone of voice, looks, acts, habits are the upper threads: and the passing moment is the shuttle swiftly, ceaselessly, relentlessly, weaving those threads into a web, and that web is life. It is woven, not by our wishing, or willing, but irresistibly, unavoidably, woven by what we *are,* moment by moment, hour after hour. What is your life weaving out? Is it attractive because of the power in it of *His* presence? Would you have it so? Would you know the secret of a life marked by the strange beauty of humility, and fragrant with the odor of *His* presence? Wait just a moment.

The *fifth* essential is a passion for winning others one by one to the Lord Jesus. A passion, I say. I may use no weaker word than that. A passion burning with the steady flame of anthracite. A passion for *winning:* not driving, nor dragging, but drawing men. I am not talking about preachers just now, as preachers, but about every one of us. Do you know the peculiar delight there is in winning the fellow by your side, the girl in your social circle, to Jesus Christ? No? Ah, you have missed half your life! Would you have such an intense passion as that, thrilling your heart, and inspiring your life, and know how to do it skillfully and tactfully?

Let me tell you with my heart that the secret not only of this, but of all four of these essentials I have named lies in the first one which I have not yet named, and grows out of it. Given the first the others will follow as day follows the rising sun.

What is the first great essential? It is this—the unrestrained, unhindered, controlling presence in the heart of the Holy Spirit. It is allowing Jesus' other Self, the Holy Spirit, to take full possession and maintain a loving but absolute monopoly of all your powers.

TARRY

My friend, have you received this promised power? Is there a growing up of those four things within you by His grace? Does the Holy Spirit have freeness of sway in you? Are you conscious of the fullness of His love and power—conscious enough to know how much there is beyond of which you are not conscious? Does your heart say "No." Well, things may be moving smoothly in that church of which you are pastor, and in that school over which you preside. Business may be in a satisfactory condition. Your standing in society may be quite

pleasing. Your plans working out well. The family
may be growing up around you as you had hoped.
But let me say to you very kindly but very plainly
your life thus far is a failure. You have been succeeding splendidly it may be in a great many important matters, but they are *the details* and in the
main issue you have failed utterly.

And to you to-night I bring one message—the
Master's Olivet message—*"tarry ye."* No need of
tarrying, as with these disciples, for *God* to do
something. His part has been done, and splendidly
done. And He waits now upon you. But tarry until
you are willing to put out of your life what dis-
pleases Him, no matter what that may mean to
you. Tarry until your eyesight is corrected; until
your will is surrendered. Tarry that you may start
the habit of tarrying, for those two Olivet words,
"Go" and "tarry," will become the even-balancing
law of your new life. A constant going to do His
will; a continual tarrying to find out His will.
Tarry to get your ears cleared and quieted so
you can learn to recognize that low voice of His.
Tarry earnestly, steadily until that touch of power
comes to change, and cleanse, and quiet, and to
give you a totally new conception of what power
is. Then you can understand the experience of the
one who wrote:

> "My hands were filled with many things
>   That I did precious hold,
> As any treasure of a king's—
>   Silver, or gems, or gold.
> The Master came and *touched* my hands,
>   (The scars were in His own)

And at His feet my treasures sweet
    Fell shattered, one by one.
'I must have empty hands,' said He,
'Wherewith to work My works through thee.'

"My hands were stained with marks of toil,
    Defiled with dust of earth;
And I my work did ofttimes soil,
    And render little worth.
The Master came and *touched* my hands,
    (And crimson were His own)
But when, amazed, on mine I gazed,
    Lo! every stain was gone.
'I must have cleansed hands,' said He,
'Wherewith to work My works through thee.'

"My hands were growing feverish
    And cumbered with much care!
Trembling with haste and eagerness,
    Nor folded oft in prayer.
The Master came and *touched* my hands,
    (With healing in His own)
And calm and still to do His will
    They grew—the fever gone.
'I must have quiet hands,' said He,
'Wherewith to work My works for Me.'

"My hands were strong in fancied strength,
    But not in power divine,
And bold to take up tasks at length,
    That were not His but mine.
The Master came and *touched* my hands,
    (And might was in His own!)
But mine since then have powerless been,
    Save His are laid thereon.
'And it is only thus,' said He,
'That I can work My works through thee.'"

The Channel

of Power

A Word that Sticks and Stings

I suppose everyone here can think of three or four persons whom he loves or regards highly, who are not christians. Can you? Perhaps in your own home circle, or in the circle of your close friends. They may be nice people, cultured, lovable, delightful companions, fond of music and good books, and all that; but this is true of them, that they do not trust and confess Jesus as a personal Savior. Can you think of such persons in your own circle? I am going to wait a few moments in silence while you recall them to mind, if you will— Can you see their faces? Are their names clear to your minds?

Now I want to talk with you a little while tonight, not about the whole world, but just about these three or four dear friends of yours. I am going to suppose them lovely people in personal contact, cultured, and kindly, and intelligent, and of good habits even though all that may not be true of all of them. And, I want to ask you a question —God's question—about them. You remember God put His hand upon Cain's arm, and, looking into his face, said: "Where is Abel, thy brother?" I want to ask you that question. Where are these four friends? Not where are they socially, nor financially, nor educationally. These are important questions. But they are less important than this other question: Where are they as touching *Him*? Where are they as regards the best life here, and the longer life beyond this one?

And I shall not ask you what you think about it. For I am not concerned just now with what you think. Nor shall I tell you what I think. For I am not here to tell you what I think, but to bring a message from the Master as plainly and kindly as I can. So I shall ask you to notice what this old book of God says about these friends of yours. It is full of statements regarding them. I can take time for only a few.

Turn, for instance, to the last chapter of Mark's Gospel, and the sixteenth verse, and you will find these words: "He that believeth and is baptized shall be saved; he that believeth not shall be—." You know the last word of that sentence. It is an ugly word. I dislike intensely to think it, much less repeat it. It is one of those blunt, sharp, Anglo-Saxon words that stick and sting. I wish I had a tenderer tone of voice, in which to repeat it, and then only in a low whisper—it is so awful— *"damned."*

Let me ask you very gently: Does the first part of that sentence—"he that believeth—trusteth—

not," does that describe the four friends you are thinking of now? And please remember that that word "believeth" does not mean the assent of the mind to a form of creed: never that: but the assent of the heart to a person: always that. "Yes," you say, "I'm afraid it does: that is just the one thing. He is thoughtful and gentlemanly; she is kind and good; but they do not trust Jesus Christ personally." Then let me add, very kindly, but very plainly, if the first part is an accurate description of your friends, the second part is meant to apply to them, too, would you not say? And that is an awful thing to say.

What a strange book this Bible is! It makes such radical statements, and uses such unpleasant words that grate on the nerves, and startle the ear. No *man* would have dared of himself to write such statements.

I remember one time visiting a friend in Boston, engaged in christian work there; an earnest man. We were talking one day about this very thing and I recall saying: "Do you really believe that what the Bible says about these people can be true? Because if it is you and I should be tremendously stirred up over it." And I recall distinctly his reply, after a moment's pause, "Well, their condition certainly will be unfortunate." *Unfortunate!* That is the Bostonese of it. That is a much less disagreeable word. It has a smoother finish—a sort of polish—to it. It does not jar on your feelings so. But this book uses a very different word from that, a word that must grate harshly upon every ear here.

I know very well that some persons have asso-

ciated that ugly word with a scene something like
this: They have imagined a man standing with fist
clenched, and eyes flashing fire, and the lines of his
face knotted up hard, as he says in a harsh voice,
"He that believeth not shall be damned," as though
he found pleasure in saying it. If there is *one* person here to-night who ever had such a conception,
will you kindly cut it out of your imagination at
once? For it is untrue. And put in its place the true
setting of the word.

Have you ever noticed what a difference the
manner, and expression of face, and tone of voice,
yes, and the character of a person make in the
impression his words leave upon your mind? Now
mark. It is Jesus talking here. *Jesus*—the tenderest-
hearted, the most mother-hearted man this world
ever listened to. Look at Him, standing there on
that hilltop, looking out toward the great world He
has just died for, with the tears coming into His
eyes, and His lips quivering with the awfulness of
what He was saying—"he that believeth not shall
be damned," as though it just broke his heart to say
it. And it did break His heart that it might not be
true of us. For He died literally of a broken heart,
the walls of that great, throbbing muscle burst
asunder by the strain of soul. That is the true setting of that terrific statement.

Please notice it does not say that God damns
men. You will find that nowhere within the pages
of this book. But it is love talking; love that sees
the end of the road and speaks of it. And true love
tells the truth at all risks when it must be told.
And Jesus because of His dying and undying love
seeks to make men acquainted with the fact which
He sees so plainly, and *they* do not.

Now turn for a moment to a second statement. You will find it in Galatians, third chapter, tenth verse. Paul is quoting from the book of Deuteronomy these words: "Cursed"—there is another ugly word—"cursed is everyone who continueth not in all the words of the book of this law to do them." Let me ask: Does that describe your friends? Well, I guess it describes us all, does it not? Who is there here that has continued in all the words of the book of this law to do them? If there is some one I think perhaps you would better withdraw, for I have no message for you to-night. The sole difference between some of us, and these friends you have in your mind is that *we* are depending upon Another who bore the curse for us. But these friends decline to come into personal touch with Him. Do they not? And this honest spoken book of God tells us plainly of that word "cursed" which has been written, and remains written, over their faces and lives.

The Bible is full of such statements. There is no need of multiplying them. And I am sure I have no heart in repeating any more of them. But I bring you these two for a purpose. This purpose: of asking you one question—whose fault is it? Who is to blame? Some one is at fault. There is blame somewhere. This thing is all wrong. It is no part of God's plan, and when things go wrong, some one is to blame. Now I ask you: *Who* is to blame?

A MOTHER-HEART

Well, there are just four persons, or groups of persons concerned. There is God; and Satan; and these friends we are talking about; and ourselves,

who are not a bit better in ourselves than they—not
a bit—but who are trusting some One else to see
us through. Somewhere within the lines of those
four we must find the blame of this awful state of
affairs. Well, we can say very promptly that Satan
is to blame. He is at the bottom of it all. And that
certainly is true, though it is not all of the truth.
Then it can be added, and added in a softer voice
because the thing is so serious, and these friends
are dear to us, that these people themselves are to
blame. And that is true, too. Because they *choose*
to remain out of touch with Him who died that it
might not be so. For there is no sin charged where
there is no choice made. Sin follows choice. Only
where one has known the wrong and has chosen
it is there sin charged.

But that this awful condition goes on unchanged
that those two ugly words remain true of our dear
friends, day after day, while we meet them, and
live with them, is there still blame? There are just
two left out of the four: God, and ourselves who
trust Him. Let me ask very reverently, but very
plainly: Is it God's fault? You and I have both
heard such a thing hinted at, and sometimes openly
said. I believe it is a good thing with reverence to
ask, and attempt to find the answer, to such a
question as that. And for answer let me first bring
to you a picture of the God of the Old Testament
whom some people think of as being just, but
severe and stern.

Away back in the earliest time, in the first book,
Genesis, the sixth chapter, and down in verses five
and six are these words: "And the Lord saw that
the wickedness of man was great in the earth,

and"—listen to these words—"that every imagination of the thoughts of his heart was only evil
continually."

What an arraignment! "Every imagination,"
"evil," *only* evil;" no mixture of good at all;
"only evil *continually*," no occasional spurts of good
even—the whole fabric bad, and bad clear through,
and all the time. Is not that a terrific arraignment?
But listen further: "And it repented the Lord that
He had made man on the earth, and"—listen to
these last pathetic words—*"it grieved Him at His
heart."*

Will you please remember that "grieve" is always
a love word? There can be no grief except where
there is love. You may annoy a neighbor, or vex a
partner, or anger an acquaintance, but you cannot
grieve except where there is love, and you cannot
be grieved except wherein you love.

I have sometimes, more often than I could wish,
seen a case like this. A young man of good family
sent away to college. He gets in with the wrong
crowd, for they are not all angels in colleges yet,
quite. Gets to smoking and drinking and gambling,
improper hours, bad companions, and all that. His
real friends try to advise him, but without effect.
By and by the college authorities remonstrate with
him, and he tries to improve, but without much
success after the first pull. And after a while, very
reluctantly, he is suspended, and sent home in dis-
grace. He feels very bad, and makes good resolu-
tions and earnest promises, and when he returns he
does do much better for a time. But it does not
last long. Soon he is in with the old crowd again,
the old round of habits and dissipations, only now

it gets worse than before; the pace is faster. And
the upshot of it all is that he is called up before the
authorities and expelled, sent home in utter dis-
grace, not to return.

And here is his chum who roomed with him, ate
with him, lived with him. He says, "Well, I declare, I am all broken up over Jim. It's too bad!
He was 'hail-fellow, well met,' and now he has
gone like that. I'm awfully sorry. It's too bad! too
bad!!" And by and by he forgets about it except
as an unpleasant memory roused up now and then.
And here is one of his professors who knew him
best perhaps, and liked him. "Well," he says, "it
is too bad about young Collins. Strange, too, he
came of good family; good blood in his veins; and
yet he seems to have gone right down with the rag-
tag. It's too bad! too bad!! I am so sorry." And
the matter passes from his mind in the press of
duties and is remembered only occasionally as one
of the disagreeable things to be regretted, and perhaps philosophized over.

And there is the boy's father's partner, down in
the home town. "Well," he soliloquizes, "it is too
bad about Collins' boy. He is all broken up over
it, and no wonder. Doesn't it seem queer? That
boy has as good blood as there is: good father,
lovely mother, and yet gone clean to the bad, and
so young. It is too bad! I am awfully sorry for
Collins." And in the busy round of life he forgets,
save as a bad dream which will come back now and
then.

But down in that boy's home there is a woman
—a mother, heartbroken—secretly bleeding her
heart out through her eyes. She goes quietly, faith-

fully about her round of life, but her hair gets
thinner, and the gray streaks it plainer, her form
bends over more, and the lines become more deeply
bitten in her face, as the days come and go. And if
you talk with her, and she will talk with you, she
will say, "Oh, yes, I know other mothers' boys go
wrong; some of them going wrong all the time; but
to think of *my Jim*—that I've nursed, and loved so,
and done everything for—to think that my Jim—"
and her voice chokes in her throat, and she refuses
to be comforted. *She grieves at her heart.* Ah! that
is the picture of God in that Genesis chapter. He
saw that the world He had made and lavished all
the wealth of His love upon had gone wrong, and
it grieved Him at His heart.

This world is God's prodigal son, and He is
heartbroken over it. And what has He done about
it. Ah! what has He done! Turn to Mark's twelfth
chapter, and see there Jesus' own picture of His
Father as He knew Him. In the form of a parable
He tells how His Father felt about things here. He
sent man after man to try and win us back, but
without effect, except that things got worse. Then
Jesus represents God talking with Himself. "What
shall I do next, to win them back?—there is My
son—My only boy—Jesus—I believe—yes, I believe I'll send Him—then they'll *see* how badly I
feel, and how much I love them; that'll touch them
surely; I'll do it." You remember just how that sixth
verse goes, "He had yet one, a beloved Son; He sent
Him *last* unto them, saying, they will *reverence* my
Son." And you know how they treated God's Son,
His love gift. And I want to remind you to-night
that, speaking in our human way—the only way we

can speak—God suffered more in seeing His Son
suffer than though He might have suffered Himself. Ask any mother here: Would you not gladly
suffer pain in place of your child suffering if you
could? And every mother-heart answers quickly,
"Aye, ten times over, if the child could be spared
pain." Where did you get that marvelous mother-
heart and mother-love? Ah, that mother-heart is a
bit of the God-heart transferred. That is what God
is like. Let me repeat very reverently that God
suffered more in giving His Son to suffer than
though He had Himself suffered. And that is the
God of the Old Testament! Let me ask: Is *He* to
blame? Has He not done His best?

Let it be said as softly as you will, and yet very
plainly, that those awful words, "damned" and
"cursed," whatever their meaning may be, are true
of your friends. Then add: It is not so because of
God's will in the matter, but in spite of His will.
Remember that God exhausted all the wealth of His
resource when He gave His Son. There can come
nothing more after that.

YOUR PERSONALITY NEEDED

Then there is a second question from God's side
to ask about those ugly words: thoughtfully, and
yet plainly—Is it the fault of Jesus, the Son of
God? And let anyone listen to Him speaking in
that tenth chapter of John. "I lay down My life for
the sheep. No man taketh it from Me. I lay it down
of Myself. I have power to lay it down and power
to take it again." And then go out yonder to that
scene just outside the Jerusalem wall. There hangs

Jesus upon that cross, suspended by nails through hands and feet. He is only thirty-three. He is intensely human. Life was just as sweet to Him that day as it is to you and me to-night. Aye, more sweet: for sin had not taken the edge off his relish of life. Plainly He could have prevented them. For many a time had He held the murderous mob in check by the sheer power of His presence alone. Yet there He hangs from nine until noon and until three—six long hours. And He said He did it for you, for me. Do not ask me to tell *how* His dying for us saves. I do not know. No one statement seems to tell all the truth. When I study into it I always get clear beyond my depth. In a tremendous way it tells a double story; of the damnable blackness of sin; and of the intensity of love. I do know that *He said* He did it for us, and for our salvation, and that it had to be done. But as we look to-day on that scene, again the question: does any of the blame of the awful statements this book makes regarding your friends belong to Him, do you think? And I think I hear your hearts say "surely not."

Well, the Father has done His best. No blame surely attaches there. The Son has gone to the utmost limit. No fault can be found there. There is just one other left up yonder, of the divine partnership—the Holy Spirit. What about Him? Listen. Just as soon as the Son went back home with face and form all scarred from His brief stay upon the earth, He and the Father said, "now We will send down the last one of Us, the Holy Spirit, and He will do His best to woo men back," and so it was done. The last supreme effort to win men

back was begun. The Holy Spirit came down for
the specific purpose of telling the world about
Jesus. His work down here is to convict men of
their terrible wrong in rejecting Jesus, and of His
righteousness, and of the judgment passed upon
Satan. Only He can convince men's minds and
consciences. A thousand preachers with the logic
of a Paul and the eloquence of an Isaiah could not
convince one man of sin. Only the Spirit can do
that. But listen to me as I say very thoughtfully—
and this is the one truth I pray God to *burn* into our
hearts to-night—that to do His work among men
He needs to use men. He needs *you.* "Oh!" you say,
"it is hardly possible that you mean that: I am not
a minister: I have no special ability for christian
work: I am just an obscure, humble christian: I
have no gift in that direction." Listen with your
heart while I remind you that He needs not your
special abilities or gifts, though He will use all you
have, and the more the better, but *He needs your
personality as a human channel* through which
to touch the men you touch. And I want to say just
as kindly and tenderly as I can and yet with great
plainness that if you are refusing to let Him use
you as He chooses—shall I say the unpleasant
truth?—the practical blame for those ugly words,
and the uglier truth back of them come straight
home to *you.*

That is a very serious thing to say, and so I must
add a few words to make it still more clear and
plain. The Spirit of God in working among men
seeks embodiment *in men,* through whom He acts.
The amazing truth is that not only is He willing to
enter into and fill you with His very presence, but

He seeks for, He wants, *yes, He needs your person-ality* as a channel or medium, that living in you He may be able to do His work among the men you touch even though you may not be conscious of much that He is doing through you. Is not that startling? He wants to live in your body, and speak through your lips, and look out of your eyes, and use your hands, really, actually. Have you turned your personality over to Him as completely as that?

Remember the law of God's communication with men; namely, He speaks *to* men *through* men. Run carefully through the Bible, and you will find that since the Cain disaster, which divided all men into two great groups, whenever God has a message for a man or a nation out in the world He chooses and uses a man in touch with Himself as His mes-senger.

Listen to Jesus' own words in that last night's long talk in John's Gospel, chapter fourteen, verse seventeen. Speaking about the coming Spirit, He says, "Whom the world cannot receive." That is a strange statement. Though an important part of the Spirit's great mission is to the world yet it can-not receive Him. But chapter sixteen, verses seven and eight gives the explanation: "I will send Him *unto you,* and He when He is come (unto you) will convince," and so on. That is to say, a message from God to one who has come within the circle of personal relation with Jesus—that message comes along a straight line without break or crook. But a message to one who remains outside that circle comes along an *angled* line—two lines meeting at an angle—and the point of that angle is in some christian heart. The message He sends out to the

outer circle passes through some one within the
inner circle. To make it direct and personal: He
needs to use you to touch those whom you touch.

God's Sub-Headquarters

Let me bring you a few illustrations of *how* God
uses men, though the *fact* of His using them is on
almost every page of this Bible. Back in the old
book of Judges is a peculiar expression which is not
brought out as clearly as it might be in our English
Bibles. The sixth chapter and thirty-fourth verse
might properly read: *"the Spirit of Jehovah clothed
Himself with Gideon."* It was a time of desperate
crisis in the nation. God chose this man for leadership among his fellows. If you take his life throughout you will not think him an ideal character. But
he seems to be the best available stuff there was.
He became the general guiding an army in what,
to human eyes, was a perfectly hopeless struggle.
Men saw Gideon moving about giving orders. But
this strangely significant phrase lets us into the
secret of his wise strategy and splendid victory.
"The Spirit of Jehovah clothed Himself with
Gideon." Gideon's personality was merely a suit of
clothes which God wore that day in achieving that
tremendous victory for His people. The same expression is used of Amasai, one of David's mighty
chieftains,[1] and of Zechariah, one of the priests
during Joash's reign.[2]

A New Testament illustration is found in the
book of Acts in the account of Philip and the

[1] 1 Chron. xii:18.
[2] 2 Chron. xxiv:20.

Ethiopian stranger. This devout African official had a copy of the old Hebrew Scriptures, but needed an interpreter to make plain their newly acquired significance. The Holy Spirit, *the* interpreter of Scripture, longs to help him. For that purpose He seeks out a man, of whom He has control, named Philip. He is directed to go some distance over toward the road where this man is journeying. We are told of Philip that he was "full of the Spirit." And a reading of that eighth chapter makes plain the controlling presence of the Spirit in Philip's personality. In the beginning He gives very explicit direction. "The Spirit (within Philip) said, go near, join thyself to this chariot." And at the close "the Spirit of the Lord caught away Philip."

These are a few illustrations of what seems to be a common law of God's intercourse with men. The language of the Bible throughout fits in with this same conception. Strikingly enough the same seems to be true in the opposing camp, among the forces of the Evil One. Repeatedly in the gospels we come across the startling expression—"possessed with demons," "possessed of demons," evidently speaking of men whom demons had succeeded in getting possession of, and clothing themselves with. It seems to be a law of *spirit* life that a spirit needs to be embodied in dealing with embodied beings. And God conforms to this law in His dealings with men.

My friend, will you ask your heart, has the Holy Spirit gotten possession of you like that? With reverence I repeat that He is seeking for men in whom He may set up a sort of sub-headquarters, from which He may work out as He pleases. Has He been able to do that with you? Or, have you been holding back from Him, fearing He might make some changes in you or your plans? If that is so, may I say just as kindly as these lips can speak it, but also as plainly, that then *the practical blame* for those cutting words about your friends comes straight back to *you.*

Hugh McAllister Beaver, son of the former governor of Pennsylvania, and one of the rarest christian young men that ever lived, felt impelled at a conference of students at Northfield, in '97, to tell this bit of his inner experience, though naturally reluctant to do so. While at college, arrangements were made for a series of meetings every night for a week. "One day going down the hallway of the college building," he said, "I met a boy we all called Dutchy, one of the toughest fellows in school. I said to him, 'Dutch, come to the meeting to-night.'" Instead of laughing or swearing, to Beaver's surprise, he paused a moment as though such a thing was possible, and Beaver said, "I prayed quietly to myself, and urged him to come." And he said, "Well, I guess I will." And that night to every one's surprise Dutch came to the meeting. When Beaver rose to speak, to his surprise this fellow was not simply intensely interested but his eyes were full of tears. And Beaver said "a voice as distinct as an audible voice said to me, 'Speak to Dutchy!' But *I did not.*" Again the next night Dutchy came of his own accord, and one of the boys putting his arm on Beaver's shoulder said, "Speak to Dutchy. We boys never saw him like this before." And he said he would. But *he did not.* And some time after he had a dream and thought he would not walk this earth any more. It did not trouble him except that his brother was crying. But he thought he met the Master, who looked into his face, and said, "Hugh, do you remember. I asked you to speak to Dutchy?" "Yes." "And you did not." "No." "Would you like to go back to the earth and win him?" And he finished the story by saying, "it's hard work, but he's coming now."

I wonder if the Master has ever tried to use your lips like that, and you have refused?

A prominent clergyman in New England tells this experience of his. In the course of his pastoral work he was called to conduct the funeral service of a young woman who had died quite unexpectedly. As he entered the house he met the minister in charge of the mission church, where the family attended, and asked him, "Was Mary a christian?" To his surprise a pained look came into the young man's face as he replied, "Three weeks ago I had a strong impulse to speak to her, but *I did not;* and I do not know." A moment later he met the girl's Sunday school teacher and asked her the same question. Quickly the tears came, as she said, "Two weeks ago, Doctor, a voice seemed to say to me, 'Speak to Mary,' and I knew what it meant, and I intended to, but *I did not,* and I do not know." Deeply moved by these unexpected answers, a few minutes later he met the girl's mother, and thinking doubtless to give her an opportunity to speak a word that would bring comfort to her own heart, he said quietly, "Mary was a christian girl?" The tears came quick and hot to the mother's eyes, as she sobbed out, "One week ago a voice came to me saying, 'Speak to Mary,' and I thought of it, but I did not at the time, and you know how unexpectedly she went away and I do not know.

Well, please understand me, I am not saying a word about that girl. I do not know anything to say. I would hope much and can understand that there is ground for hope. But this is what I say: How pathetic, beyond expression, that the Spirit tried to get the use of the lips of three persons, a pastor, a teacher, aye, a *mother!* to speak the word that evidently ·He longed to have spoken to her, *and He could not!*

Has He tried to use you *like that?*

THE HIGHEST LAW OF ACTION

But these two illustrations are narrower than the truth. They speak of the lips. He wants to use your lips; but, even more, He wants to use your *life.* Much as He may use your lips, He will use your personality, your presence, your life ten times more, when you are wholly unconscious of it. He loves men so much. He longs to save them. But He needs us—you and me—as channels through which His power shall flow to touch and mightily influence those whom we touch. How often has He turned away disappointed because the channel had broken connections, or could not be used?

"He was not willing that any should perish;
    Jesus, enthroned in the glory above,
Saw our poor fallen world, pitied our sorrows,
    Poured out His life for us, wonderful love.
Perishing, perishing, thronging our pathway,
    Hearts break with burdens too heavy to bear;
Jesus would save, but there's no one to tell them,
    No one to save them from sin and despair."

Someone says: "You are putting an awful responsibility upon us. Would you have us go out and begin speaking to everyone we meet?" No, that is not what I am saying just now. Though there is a truth there. But this: Surrender yourself to Jesus as your *Master*, for Him to take possession. Turn the channel over to Him, that He may tighten the connections, upward and outward, and clean it out, and then use as He may choose. He has a passion for winning men, and He has marvelous tact in doing it. Let Him have His way in you. Keep quiet and close to Him, and *obey* Him, gladly, cheerily, constantly, and *He will assume all responsibility for the results.*

There is a law of personal service. It is this: Contact means opportunity; opportunity means responsibility. To come into personal contact with a man gives an opportunity of influencing him for Christ, and with opportunity goes its twin partner —responsibility.

There is another law—a higher law—the highest law of the christian life. It is this: In everything hold yourself subject to *the Holy Spirit's leading.* Whenever these two laws come into conflict remember that the lower law always yields to the higher. It is a law of life that where two laws come into conflict the lower law always gives way to the higher. That is a supreme law both of nature and in legislation. Now, the highest law of the christian life is to yield constantly to the leading of our Companion—the Holy Spirit. Then quiet time alone with the Master daily over His word for the training of the ear, and the training of the judgment, and the training of the tongue becomes the great essential.

But to-night the great question is: Have you turned the channel of power—your personality—over to Him to be flushed and flooded with His power? Will you?

"Only a smile, yes, only a smile,
    That a woman o'erburdened with grief
    Expected from you; 'twould have given relief,
For her heart ached sore the while.
    But, weary and cheerless, she went away,
    Because, as it happened that very day,
You were *out of touch* with your Lord.

"Only a word, yes, only a word,
    That the Spirit's small voice whispered, 'Speak';
    But the worker passed onward, unblessed and weak,
Whom you were meant to have stirred
    To courage, devotion and love anew,
    Because, when the message came to you,
You were *out of touch* with your Lord.

"Only a note, yes, only a note,
    To a friend in a distant land;
    The Spirit said, 'Write,' but then you had planned
Some different work, and you thought
    It mattered little. You did not know
    'Twould have saved a soul from sin and woe—
You were *out of touch* with your Lord.

"Only a song, yes, only a song,
    That the Spirit said, 'Sing to-night;
    Thy voice is thy Master's by purchased right.'
But you thought, ' 'Mid this motley throng,
    I care not to sing of the City of God';
    And the heart that your words might have reached
        grew cold—
You were *out of touch* with your Lord.

"Only a day, yes, only a day,
   But oh! can you guess, my friend,
   Where the influence reaches and where it will end,
Of the hours that you frittered away?
   The Master's command is, 'Abide in Me';
   And fruitless and vain will your service be,
 If *out of touch* with your Lord."

The Price
of Power

Every man needs power. Every earnest man covets power. Every willing man has the Master's promise of power. But every man does not possess the promised power. And many, it is to be feared, never will. Many a man's life to-day is utterly lacking in power. Some of us will look back at the close of life with a sense of keen disappointment and of bitter defeat. And the reason is not far to seek, nor hard to see through. If we do not have power it is because *we are not willing to pay the price.*

Everything costs. There is a law of exchange that rules in every sphere of life. It is this, "to get, you must give." It rules in the business world. If I want a house or a hat I must give the sum agreed upon. It rules in the intellectual world. If a young man wants a disciplined mind he must give time, and close application, and some real, hard work. It

73

holds true in the spirit realm. If you and I wish to
have business transactions in this upper world of
spirit-life we must be governed by this same law.
To have power in our lives over sin and selfishness,
and passion, and appetite; over tongue, and temper, and self-seeking ambition; to have power in
prayer, and in winning others over from sin to
Jesus Christ, one must first lay down the required
price.

What is the price of power? Turn to Jesus' talk
with Peter and the others in the latter part of the
sixteenth chapter of Matthew's gospel. Jesus has
been telling them of the awful cross-experiences
which He clearly saw ahead. Peter probably fear-
ful that whatever came to his Master might possibly
come to himself also, and shrinking back in horror
from that, has the hardihood to rebuke Jesus. The
Master, recognizing the suggestion as coming from
a far subtler individual than Peter, who is using
ignorant Peter's selfishness to repeat the suggestion
of the wilderness, again bids *him* begone. Then in
a few simple words of far-reaching significance,
He states first the standard of power, and then the
price to be paid by one who would reach that
standard. Listen to Him: "If any man would come
after Me, let him deny himself and take up his
cross and follow Me."

In the Footprints of Jesus

Let us look a little into these familiar words. "If
any man *would come after Me*"—that is the standard set before us. Not to be regarded as a pillar in
the church, a leader in religious circles, a good

Bible student, a generous giver, an earnest speaker, an energetic worker, a spiritually minded person, but, what *may* not be coupled with any or all of these admirable things, *to tread in the footprints of Jesus.*

Think back into that marvelous life. A human life, remember. For though He was Son of God He lived His life down here as a son of man. Think of His power over temptation, not alone at the outset in the fierce wilderness struggle, but through those succeeding years of intense conflict; His power over Satan, over man-possessing demons, over disease; His power in dealing with the subtle schoolmen trying their best to trip Him up, as well as over His more violent enemies who would have dashed Him over yon Nazareth precipice, or later stoned the life out of His body in Jerusalem. Recall the power of His rare unselfishness; His combined plainness and tenderness of speech in dealing with men; His unfailing love to all classes; His power as a soul winner, as a man of prayer, as a popular preacher, lovingly wooing men while unsparingly rebuking their sins. *There* is the suggestion of Jesus' standard of power. Would you go *after Him?* You may. For as the Father sent Him even so sends He us, to do the same work and live the same life.

But wait a moment before answering that question. There is another side in His life to that "come-after-me." Opposites brought into contact produce a violent disturbance. Such a life as that of Jesus, down in the atmosphere of this world will of necessity provoke bitter enmities, both then and now. Listen. He was criticized and slandered. They said He was peculiar and fanatical. His friends thought Him "beside Himself," swept off His feet by excessive, hot-headed enthusiasm. They "laughed Him to scorn," and reviled Him. They picked His words, and nagged His kindliest acts, and dogged His steps. Repeated attempts were made upon His life, both at Nazareth and by stoning at Jerusalem. A determined conspiracy against His life was planned by the Jerusalem officials six months before the end actually came. He was practically a fugitive for those months. At the last He was arrested and mocked and *spit* upon, struck with open hand and clenched fist, derisively crowned with thorns, and finally killed—a cruel, lingering, tortured death.

"If any man would *come after Me*." Plainly this language of Jesus put back into its original setting begins to assume a new significance.

A Fixed Purpose

But look at these words a little more closely. "If"—it is an open question, this matter of following Jesus. It is kept open by many people who want to be known as christian, but who hesitate over what a plain understanding of Jesus' words may involve. Some of us may be disposed to shrink back from the simple meaning these words will yet disclose.

"If any man *would*"—would is the past tense of will. The word will is one of the strongest in our language. A man's will is the imperial part of him. It is the autocrat upon the throne; the judge upon the bench of final appeal. Jesus is getting down to

the root of matters here. He is appealing to the
highest authority. No mere passing sentiment is
this. Not attending a meeting and being swept
along with the crowd by the hour's influence. But
a fixed purpose, calmly, resolutely settled upon,
rooted away down deep in the very vitals of the will
to follow Jesus absolutely, no matter what it may
cost or where it may cut.

I wonder how many of us would form such a
purpose, to follow Jesus *blindly*, utterly regardless
of what it might be found to mean as the days come
and go? "Oh, well," I hear some one say, "why
talk like that. Nobody is required to suffer to-day
as He did." Do you think not? I am not so sure
about that. There is a young man in Southern
India, bright fellow, full of power, of high class
family, who heard of Jesus, and felt the personal
appeal to himself of that marvelous story. He
thought a good while of what it meant, and what it
might involve, and at length resolutely formed his
decision to accept and follow Jesus. As he had
anticipated, his dear ones remonstrated with him,
coaxed, pleaded, threatened, and finally, his own
father violently put him out of his life-long home,
and he has remained since *an outcast* from home
and loved ones. These words of Jesus surely are
full of significance to him.

"But that was in India, far off, heathen India,"
you say. Well, here is something of a similar sort
at home. I knew a young woman in a certain New
England town visiting away from home. She attended some meetings where she was visiting, and
decided to be a christian. She was betrothed to a
young man, not a christian, in her home town. At

once she wrote him explaining her new step thinking, doubtless, how glad he would be. For most men
seem very willing to have their *wives* christian.
But he wrote back that if she were determined to
be a christian that must put an end to their engage-
ment. He was not a christian and did not want
his wife to be one. Every one here must know how
serious a question that brought up for decision.
For she was a true woman, and love's tendrils twine
with wondrous tenacity about a woman's heart.
And I presume, too, that everyone of you has already thought while I am speaking, of the temptation that, quick as a flash, went through her mind.
"You need not make a public matter of this. Just
be a true christian in heart and life, and in that
way *you'll win him over afterwards.*" I imagine
some of you have heard something like that before.
But she remembered that her new Master said
"Confess" as well as "believe." It was a crisis; a
severe struggle of soul. But she felt she must follow
her Master's leading regardless of what it involved.
And so she decided. You are not surprised to know
that she was ill for a time. The intense strain of
spirit affected her body. "If—any—man—would—
come—after—Me" meant much to her. Did it not?

Without doubt if some of *us* listening to-day
were to follow Jesus quietly, but absolutely, in all
things as His own Spirit plainly led, we would find
as sharp a line of separation drawn against us, as
did He in Palestine, and these young people in
India and America.

Many a social door would be shut in our faces.
O, shut *politely* of course! Society thinks it in very
bad form to get unduly excited about mere matters

of religious opinion. But the door is *shut,* and barred, too. Some of us would possibly be searching for other business positions before to-morrow's light faded away if we were determined to go only where *He* clearly pointed the way.

But we have only begun to get at the meaning of Jesus' words. Is there still *a fixed purpose* to follow regardless of what meaning these words may yet disclose? Not impossibly the company of those willing to go straight through this verse with a calm, determined "yes" to every word of Jesus, will grow smaller as we go on.

A Character Sketch

Let us go a little farther. "If any man would come after Me let him *deny himself.*" "Deny himself"—what does that mean? Well, deny means to say "no," plainly and positively. Himself is the smoother English word for his self. Let him say "no" to his self. Please notice that Jesus is not speaking of what is commonly called self-denial. That is, repressing some desire for a time, sacrificing something temporarily in order to gain an advantage later. That sort of thing is not peculiar to the christian life, but is practiced by all classes, even among the lowest. He is not speaking of that, but of something far more radical. Reading the verse through again, it will be seen that there are three distinct persons referred to by Jesus. First, the "any man" He speaks of, and then the two others represented by these words "himself" and "Me," either one or the other of whom is influencing this "any man's" life. "Say no to his self"

is coupled with "follow Me." And the opposite is
implied—if any man will not do as *I* desire, he
will continue to do as he is now doing, namely,
deny Me and follow his self.

These two persons self and Jesus are placed
here in sharpest contrast. An uncompromising
antagonism exists between them. They are sworn
foes, and every man must decide to which he will
yield his allegiance. To agree with either one is to
oppose the other one. For a man to settle some
matter that comes up for decision by saying "yes"
to the desires or demands of his self involves his
saying "no" to Jesus. And on the other hand his
yielding assent to the plans and wishes of this
"me," namely Jesus, is plainly equivalent to saying
"no" to his self.

What is this self in each of us that Jesus sets in
such antagonism to Himself, and instructs us to say
a hard, uncompromising, unceasing "no" to? There
are a few words in common use that give some suggestion of its character. There is the word selfish,
that is, being absorbed in one's own self; in getting
every stream to flow by his own door. That is
commonly regarded, even in absolutely worldly
circles, as a detestable trait. Its opposite, self-for-
getful, being full of forgetting one's self in thinking
of others, is as commonly regarded in all circles as
a charming, winsome trait of character. The words
self-centered, and self-willed, are as familiar and
suggestive.

The fact is, there is an individual living inside
each one of us whom Jesus refers to, by this word
"his self." This individual takes on the degree of
intensity and other local coloring of the person it

inhabits. It may be polished, scholarly, cultured; or, coarse, ignorant and ill-mannered. But "scratch a Russian and you find a Tartar." Scratch through the veneering here and, whether coarse or highly polished, you will find the same individual—self.

There are some quite marked characteristics by which its presence may be recognized. They may not all be noticeable together in any one person. But one or more will be found in every person whom it succeeds in influencing and dominating. One characteristic is this: *it covets praise*. It feeds and fattens on commendation. It constantly seeks to be highly esteemed, to have its worth properly appraised. It is immensely impressed with its own importance, its value to society, its keenness, wisdom or aptness, and wishes others to be so impressed also. It is fond of a mirror, especially one made to magnify. It seeks recognition. It presses forward, rudely or politely, according as its habitat has been trained in rude or polite circles. It may put on the garb of humility, and use the language of depreciation. But its ear is none the less keenly alert to hear the agreeable things and to cherish them.

Another characteristic, which really is simply the other side of this first named one, is this: *it shrinks from criticism*. How it writhes and twists at the least touch of unfavorable criticism! It is always on the defensive. The cheek colors at the suggestion of its being wrong, or having blundered, or of being peculiar.

How quickly it explains and defends and brings evidence of its being in the right. It is extremely sensitive. "It is that *touchy* thing in you." It is

chronically troubled with "the disease of *touchi-
ness.*" Its feelings are readily hurt. It is easily
slighted. It remembers grievances. It has an inter-
rogation point constantly on sentinel duty, namely,
What will *they* think? What will *they* say? It lives
in constant fear, under the lash of that huge,
vague, awful *they*.

I remember knowing a Sunday school teacher
who had a mission class of rather rough boys from
non-christian homes. I asked one day how she was
getting along with them. "Going to give them up,"
she replied. "Is that so? They have all become
christians?" No, none of them were christians,
and they liked her, and said they would not come
if she gave them up, but she felt discouraged, and
anyway she had decided to give them up. Lawyers
and women do not always give their reasons, very
wisely. I ventured to suggest that before giving
them up, she have the boys come up to her home,
one at a time, perhaps for tea; have a pleasant chatty time at tea and afterwards, and then
before the boy left have a quiet friendly talk with
him by himself about being a christian, and, a few
words of prayer with him. Wouldn't she try that
before giving them up? And I remember distinctly
that her face blushed as red as a bright red rose, as
she replied, "Why, Mr. Gordon, he'd *laugh at me!*"
And she could not bear the possible chance of being
laughed at for the other more likely possibility of
winning a soul—a man—a life. That was "self"
in her, shrinking back from a laugh; dreading that
look of possibly contemptuous surprise that *might*
come.

Another person, speaking about certain recreations very common in society, and which he was in the habit of joining, though freely questioning the propriety of so doing, said, "O, I don't care much for those things. I could easily give them up, but people think you are so queer if you decline, and you feel as if you were a back number." Ah! there was the rub. The desire to be thought well of; the dislike of being considered peculiar; the fear of that thinly veiled sneering curl on the lip—that was *self* in him asserting its presence, and even more, ruling his action. Do you recognize the individual inside of you that Jesus is speaking of?

There is a third tell-tale earmark of self that is difficult to conceal—*it is assertive*. It dearly loves to have its own way. It has plans and ambitions, and proposes to carry them through regardless of man, or—let the plain truth be spoken softly—of God. Its opinions are held tenaciously. Its favorite pronoun is I, capitalized, with variations of my and me. The personal equation is extremely powerful and persuasive.

The true follower of Jesus holds every plan subject to change from above. But this self, if allowed to rule, takes the bit in its tightly-shut teeth, and drives determinedly ahead, reckless of either man's or God's preferences, even though religious phraseology may be upon its tongue.

Still another trait of character of this self whose closer acquaintance we are making is this: *It has an insatiable appetite*. It grows hungrier by that on which it feeds. Its capacity is beyond the measuring line. If given free rein it will debase the holiest functions of the body, and degrade the highest powers of the mind to appease its gnawing, passion-bitten hunger. The noblest gifts, the purest emotions, the most sacred relationships, are dragged down to the slimy gutter to tempt and temporarily stay its jaded palate.

Unmasked

That is something of a suggestion of the character of this other master than Jesus, who seeks to get control of us, and from whose relentless, vise-like grip Jesus would fain free us. He says there is only one thing to do with it. No halfway compromise—the great American expedient—will do here. The Master says plainly it is to be denied, repressed, put determinedly down, starved, strangled. To every suggestion or demand there is to be a prompt, positive, jaw-locked no.

There is war to the knife, and the knife clear up to the hilt, between these two claimants for the control of our powers—self and Jesus. Paul understood this antagonism thoroughly. It comes out repeatedly in his writings. His name for this inner enemy, by an accidental turn in English, is Jesus' word "self" spelled backwards with the letter "h" added —f-l-e-s-h. His remarks in Romans, eighth chapter, verses four to eight, and twelve to thirteen, are simply an enlargement of these words in the sixteenth of Matthew's gospel. If one will read these verses, substituting Jesus' word "self" for Paul's word he will be surprised to find how strikingly Paul is expressing this very thought of Jesus. A free translation of part of these verses would read like this: Verse five—"They that choose to walk after self (as a slave walked after, or behind, his master)

will show their choice by obeying the desires of
self, and they that choose to walk after the Spirit
will obey the desires of the Spirit." Verse seven—
"For the purposes of self are opposed to God's
purposes; for it does not hold itself subject to
God's wishes; indeed, in its very nature it cannot;
and they that choose to obey self cannot please
God." Verse thirteen—"If by the Holy Spirit's aid ye
kill off the plans and doings of self, ye shall therein
find real true life, and only so."

Plainly, the deep searching experiences of Paul's
great soul, and his wide observation of others, in
his ceaseless travels, confirm the statements already made, that there is the intensest hatred, the
bitterest antagonism, between these two personali-
ties represented by Jesus' words, "himself" and
"me." There can be no patched-up truce here. The
only way the lion and the lamb can lie down
together in this case is for the one to lie down
underneath the other—conquered; or inside the
other—devoured.

In his other letters Paul sometimes uses still
another name, "the old man," and names the characteristics of this omnipresent self, which crop out
with varying degrees of prominence, in different
persons, and under different circumstances. Notice
only a few of these: In Galatians, fifth chapter,
nineteenth verse: "The deeds of self are . . .
improper sexual intercourse, impurity, shameless
looseness. . . ." It will, wherever possible, debase
the holiest functions of the body. In Colossians,
third chapter, fifth verse, speaking of the "old
man": "And covetousness, which is reckoning of
highest worth that which is less worthy than God."

That is to say, the ambitious longings of self, will if unchecked become the ruling passion, thrusting all else ruthlessly aside and degrading the highest powers of the mind to satisfying its feverish desire. In Ephesians, fourth chapter, thirty-first verse: "Bitterness, passion, anger, loud disputing, evil-speaking . . . malice." Its assertiveness, and demand for a due recognition of its worth, its rights, its opinions, its proper place, bring bitterest burnings, and worse. It will not be needful to review congressional, and political, and society life for illustrations. They may be found much nearer one's own door.

Was there ever such a list? Such a being whose heart begets and nurses such progeny! This being has the smell of hell, and of the evil one himself. Ah! now we are getting at the straight truth. Self is Satan's personal representative in every human heart. Its door of entrance is the door of disobedience. It can have control only where one allows himself to get out of intelligent sympathy with God. The self in Peter was recoiling from that cross of which Jesus spoke. How keen Jesus was in recognizing the suggestor of the thought that found expression through Peter's lips—"Get thee behind me, *Satan*." Self is Satan, condensed into each man's life, though in some he dare not exhibit his coarser traits; and in others he is being *constantly conquered* by that power of the Spirit of Jesus which comes through absolute, glad surrender to Him.

This sly Satan-self may often be recognized by a favorite question it asks among christian people about a great many so-called unimportant matters:

—What's the harm? But a true follower of Jesus never lives down upon the plane of "what's-the-harm?" He lives up in a higher sphere with his Master, who "pleased not Himself," but made it the steady, unfaltering aim of His life to do always those things that were pleasing to His Father. Men thought Him narrow and fanatical, but He cared not so long as He could daily hear that clear, sweet voice saying "This is My beloved Son, in whom I am well pleased." The final touchstone which the follower of Jesus applies to every matter is this: *Would it please Him?*

Let everyone here who earnestly desires to fit into, and to fill out, Jesus' plan for his life, take paper and pencil and make a list of his personal habits; such as his eating, what he eats and how; his drinking, other things he puts into his mouth, his dress, the use and care of his body, his recreations, his reading, his conversation, his use of money, his use of time, his life plans and his daily plans, his social engagements; and regarding each ask plainly the question—what is the *motive* that *controls* me in this? Is it my own preference or enjoyment? Or, is it to please and honor Jesus? Let him further go through the list of his business methods, his friendships, the various organizations he belongs to, with the same question. If he will do thorough work he will probably have some stiff fighting on hand both at the start and afterwards. Many a life would thereby be radically changed. For example, I know a christian storekeeper who has on his shelves a certain article bearing the label of a tonic medicine, but he knows perfectly well, as does anyone who stops to think about it, that the

stuff back of the label is one form of an intoxicant.
There can be no question of what the Master would
say about it. But it brings a good profit. And his
money-fevered self asserts its mastery and carries
the day. And the man tightly grips the profits,
while Satan chuckles with unholy glee, and souls
are being damned by this christian man's aid. Certainly there can be none of the power of God in
such a life. Let us rather speak the truth and say
that this man is exerting a positive power for Satan
and for hell.

All this is included in these few simple words,
"let him deny himself." Is there still a fixed purpose to follow Jesus without regard to what it may
cost us, or where the keen edge of separation may
cut in?

THE BATTLE OF THE FORKS

Here is a forking of the road. I bring this whole
company up to this dividing, and therefore de-
ciding, point. Let each choose his own road
deliberately, prayerfully, with open eyes. This road
to the left has as its law, yielding to self; saying
"yes" to the desires and demands of self; with some
modifications possibly, here and there, for I am
talking to professing christian people. Yes to Jesus
sometimes, but at *other* times, when it suits circumstances and inclinations better to do otherwise
—well, a pushing of the troublesome question
aside. And that means a decided yes to self, with
as positive a negative to Jesus' desires implied
thereby. That is the left-hand fork.

This right-hand road knows only one law to

which exception is never made, namely: *Yes to Jesus*, everywhere, always, regardless of consequences, though it may entail loss of friendships, or money, or position, or social standing, or personal preference, or radical change of plans, or, what not.

Judas assented to the craving of his ambitious self and said "no" to his Master, thinking possibly, with his worldly shrewdness, thereby to force Jesus to assert His power. He little knew what a time of crisis it was, and what terrific results would follow.

Peter stood on the side of his cowardly, shrinking self in the court-yard that dark night, and against his Master. And though with matchless love he was forgiven, he never forgave himself, nor was able to get that night's doings out of his memory. Judas and Peter were brothers in action that night, and there are evidences that many other disciples are standing over in the same group. Are you? Which road do you choose to-night: this—to the left? Or, this—to the right?

I knew a young man who was deeply attached to an admirable young woman, both refined christian persons, much above the average in native ability, and in culture. He made known to her his feelings. But as many a woman who does not trust her best Friend in such matters is apt to do she held him off, testing him repeatedly, to find out just how real his attachment was. Finally revealing indirectly her own feeling she still withheld the consent he pleaded for, until he would yield acquiescence in a certain plan of hers for him. The plan, proper enough in itself, was an ambitious one, and tended decidedly toward swinging him away from the

high, tenderly spiritual ideals that had swayed his
life in college and afterwards, though he probably
was not clearly conscious of this tendency. The
only safe thing to do under such strong circumstances was to take time, aside, alone, for calm,
poised, thought and prayer, to learn if her plan
was also the Master's plan for him. But the personal element proved too strong for such deliberation. The possibility of losing her swung him off his
feet. It was no longer a question between her plan
and the Master's plan. The latter dropped out of
view, probably half-unconsciously because hur-
riedly. *He must have her,* he thought. That rose
before his eyes above all else. And so the decision
was made. With what result? He is to-day prominent in christian service, an earnest speaker, a tire-
less worker, with a most winsome personality. But
his inner spiritual life has perceptibly dwarfed. His
ideals, still high and noble, are distinctly lower
than in his earlier life. Intellectual ideals, admirable in themselves, but belonging in second place
in a christian life, now command the field. His
conceptions and understandings of spiritual truth
have undergone a decided change.

The proposal of the self-life came in very fascinating guise to him. He hastily said "yes" to it:
that meant as decided a refusal of Another's plan
for him, which had once been clearly recognized,
and accepted, but was now set aside, be it sadly
said, as he swung quickly off to the left fork of
the road.

There is an incident told of a European pastor,
an earnest, eloquent man. The realization came in
upon him that he had not been fully following the

Master. In much of his life self was still ruling.
He came to this forking of the road, and the battle
was a fierce one, for self dies hard. But finally "by
the Spirit," he got the victory, as every one may,
and calmly stepped off to the right. He has vividly
described that battle of the forks in language, the
accuracy of which will be recognized by others who
have been in action on that field.

> "Oh, the bitter shame and sorrow,
>   That a time could ever be
>   When I let the Saviour's pity
>   Plead in vain, and proudly answered
>   *'All of self, and none of Thee.'*
>
> "Yet He found me: I beheld him
>   Bleeding on the accursed tree;
>   Heard Him pray, 'forgive them, Father'
>   And my wistful heart said faintly,
>   *'Some of self and some of Thee.'*
>
> "Day by day, His tender mercy,
>   Healing, helping, full and free,
>   Sweet and strong, and oh, so patient,
>   Brought me lower, while I whispered:
>   *'Less of self and more of Thee.'*
>
> "Higher than the highest heaven,
>   Deeper than the deepest sea,
>   Lord, *thy love* at last has conquered;
>   Grant me now my soul's desire,
>   *'None of self and all of Thee.'* "

Is there still a fixed purpose? Will you take this
right fork? Let those who will, and those who
linger reluctantly listen to the further word that

Jesus adds: "Let him deny himself and take up his cross." *"Take up his cross"*—what does that mean? The cross has come to be regarded in these days as a fine ornament. It looks beautiful bejeweled; on the end of a sword; or worked into regalia. It makes such an artistic finish to a church building, finely chiseled in stone, or enwreathed with ivy. It looks pretty in jewelry and flowers. But to Jesus and the men of His time it had a grim, hard, painful significance. In Roman usage a man condemned to this death was required to take up the crude wooden cross provided, carry it out to the place of execution, and there be transfixed upon it. Plainly to these men listening, Jesus' words meant: Let him say "no" to his self, and then nail it up on the cross and leave it there *to die.*

Paul understood this thoroughly. To help the young christians in Galatia he explains his own experience by saying: *"I have been crucified* with Christ;" and to the unknown friends in Rome he writes: "if ye by the Spirit *put to death* the doings of the self life ye shall live." The only thing to do with this self is to kill it.

In Luke's account an intensely practical word is added to Jesus' remark: "Let him take up his cross *daily.*" A cat is said to have nine lives, because it is so hard to kill. I do not know what your experience may have been, but, judged by this rule, the self in me is tougher-lived than that. It has about ninety-nine, or nine hundred and ninety-nine lives. I put it on the cross to-day in the purpose of my will by the power of the Spirit, and I find it trying to sneak down and step into active control again to-morrow through some sly, subtle suggestion which it hopes may get past the vigilance of my sentinel. That word *daily* becomes, of necessity, my constant keynote—a *daily* conflict, a *daily* sleepless vigilance, and, thank God, a *daily* *victory*.

Every man's heart is a battlefield. If self has possession, Jesus is lovingly striving to get possession. If possession has been yielded to Jesus, there is a constant besieging by the forces of self. And self is a skilled strategist. In every heart there is a cross, and a throne, and each is occupied. If Jesus is on the throne, ruling, self is on the cross, dying. But if self is being obeyed, and so is ruling, then it is on the throne. And self on the throne means that *Jesus has been put on the cross*. And it seems to be only too pathetically true that not only in New Testament times, but in these times, there are numbers of professing christians, who, in the practice of daily life, are crucifying the Son of God afresh, and openly exposing Him to shame before the eyes of the crowd.

Suppose that to-night I determine to make this absolute surrender to Jesus as my Master. To-morrow in some manner, possibly a small matter—speaking a word to some one—asking a silent blessing at the meal—making a change in some personal habit—or some other apparently trivial matter—the Spirit quietly makes clear *His wish* as to what I should do. But I hesitate: it seems hard. I do not say that I will not obey, but actually *I do not*. Let me plainly understand that in such a single failure to obey, self is again mounting the throne, and Jesus is being dethroned and put over yonder on the cross.

Do some of us still hesitate at this forking of the roads, irresolute? A crowned Christ is attractive. But self's tendrils, though small, are tenaciously tough, and twine into so many corners and around some hidden things. And the uprooting and out-cutting mean sharp pain. Is that so? And you hesitate? Please take another frank look.

Lock-Step

These two forks differ radically. They differ in direction. One is to the *left;* the other to the *right.* And these two words are significant of more than direction. They differ in grade. This left-hand road does not seem to have any grade. It is smooth and level, and straightaway, *apparently.* But a keener look reveals a slant *down,* very slight at first, but steadily increasing, not only in its down-ward grade, but in the *proportionate* grade down.

This right-hand road has a decided grade *up* from the beginning, a steep slant, that causes many to avoid it, though they feel impelled to take it. Those who take it say that after the first decided step into it the slant does not seem nearly so hard as before starting, and that climbing it makes splendid muscle and gives an inspiring sense of exhilaration from the very start. The atmosphere is rare and purifying and invigorating. It is not traveled by so many, though the number keeps increasing. But such rare companionship, hitherto unknown, they afford!

The striking peculiarity of this road, however, is this, that each one keeps lock-step with a certain One who leads the way. This One is remarkable in

appearance. His face combines all the strength and
resolution of the strongest man's with all the fine-
ness and gentleness of the finest woman's. But He
bears peculiar marks as though He had been
through some terrible experience. His face has a
number of small scars as though it had been torn
by thorns and cut by thongs. His hands and feet
look as though huge spikes had been forced through
them. But the glory-light of another world is in His
eyes, and illumines His face radiantly, and a glad
ring is in His low, musical, singularly clear voice.

The walking in step with Him is *so* close that one
can feel the tender throbbing of His heart, and can
talk confidentially with Him in low, quiet tones,
and can hear distinctly His gentle still-like voice
in reply.

As one steps off quietly, determinedly to the right
from the battle of the forks he hears the closing
words of Jesus' remarks to Peter—*"and follow Me."*
Jesus sends no one ahead alone. He blazes out
every path through the unknown, unbroken forest,
and asks us simply to come along after Him. He
did what He asks us to do. The self-life was
alluringly and repeatedly presented to Him by
Satan, in the wilderness, in the remark of Peter, by
the visit of the Greeks, in Gethsemane where the
struggle of soul almost broke the tie that held body
and spirit together, and many other times. In many
a hard battle—for the divine Jesus was intensely
human in His earthly life—He repeatedly said a
never-varying "no" to the self-life, and lived a
constant victory until the very last triumphant
shout of victory on Calvary. It was a life of constant
conflict, but of splendid, calming, scarce-broken

peace within, and of marvelous power without.

Earnestly, lovingly, gently, yet passionately, He stands just ahead in that path now, with pierced hands outstretched in open invitation, with a heart-yearning in the depths of His great eyes, wooing us on to follow where He goes on before.

Let us follow. It may be, it *will* be, in some measure, through the experiences of the wilderness temptation, and of Gethsemane, and of Calvary, but it will also be to share the victory which was always coupled with every testing *He* met. It will as certainly be following Him in power, and victory, on past Calvary to the new life of the resurrection morning, that saw the greatest display of power. And even past that, to the upper chamber where His words burn their way into our hearts—"as the Father sent Me (clothed with power unconquerable) even so send I you." And then to Olivet where the victorious words ring out, "All power hath been given unto me in heaven and on earth, therefore go ye and make disciples."

> *"If any man*
> *would come after me,*
> *let him say "no" to his self,*
> *and nail it to the cross daily,*
> *and follow me."*

Jesus, Master, by the Holy Spirit's help, *I will.*

The Personality
of Power

A PERSONALLY CONDUCTED JOURNEY

Everyone enjoys the pleasure of travel; but nearly all shrink back from its tiresomeness and drudgery. The transportation companies are constantly scheming to overcome this disagreeable side for both pleasure and business travel. One of the popular ways of pleasure travel of late is by means of personally conducted tours. A party is formed, often by the railroad company, and is accompanied by a special agent to attend to all the business matters of the trip. A variation of this is to arrange for a group of congenial people to accompany some well-known accomplished gentleman. This gives the trip, not alone the convenience of having all business matters cared for, but also the decided enjoyment which this gentleman's wide knowledge and experience, and personal contact incidentally give. There are some criticisms however of such parties, from the standpoint of greatest comfort and of freedom in moving about.

Probably the very pleasantest way—the ideal way, to travel anywhere, either in our own home land, or abroad—is to form a party of only a very few persons, mutually congenial, and personally agreeable, *one of whom is an experienced traveler,* to whom checking baggage, buying tickets, studying time-tables, planning connections and all the rest of that sort of thing which, to most, is disagreeable drudgery, to whom all that is mere pleasant detail; and who in addition knows all the ground you will cover, the best hotels, the inconveniences to avoid, the desirable places and things, and who finds rare enjoyment in making the trip delightful and inspiring, and restful too, to these dear friends of his.

For instance if the trip is a foreign one beginning with a run through Great Britain it would add immensely to have such a friend in London who knew that great whirling world-metropolis, as you know your own home. After a bit you may slip over the Channel to Holland. It is only a few hours away, but the strange language, new customhouse rules, new usages, new sights, different sort of people, all make it a totally different world. A few hours will bring you into Sweden, or west from the hollow-landed Dutch to the higher-landed Germans, or south through Belgium into sunny France, and so on. And in each place the customs, and language, and sights, and people, the food, the sleeping arrangements, and apparently everything, especially to a stranger, are totally different. It is this very variety—the constant change of surroundings—that constitutes much of the charm of it all. There is nothing so refreshing and invigorating as that. But on the other hand to an entire stranger who has no guide, it is apt to be confusing and wearisome. And the tiresome side often overcomes the pleasant side. Now this is what I am saying, that, if there are just a few together, and this experienced traveler, who is also a dear friend, is one of them, the trip is radically changed. You move in a new world. He can talk Dutch in Holland, and German in Germany, Swedish in Scandinavia, and French in Switzerland. He sees the baggage past the customs officials, and provides restful stopping places, and keeps the disagreeables away from you. He knows the places to visit, and is familiar with the historic occurrences, and is a quiet, cheery companion, and *if* with it all he has an unlimited letter-of-credit, and makes you feel that somehow you are favoring him by letting him help you out when you run short—that, I say, would be *the ideal way of traveling.*

Now why take so much time speaking about all that? Listen! I will tell you why. Living is like traveling. Life is a journey. It is a trip through a strange land where you have never been before, and you never know a moment ahead where you are going next. Strange languages, strange scenes, strange dilemmas; new tangles, new experiences, and some old ones with new faces so you do not know them. It is just as chock-full of pleasure and enjoyment as it can be, if you could only make some provision for the drudgery and hard things that seem to crowd in so thick and fast sometimes, as to make people forget the gladness of it.

Now I have something to tell you that seems too utterly good to be believed, and yet keeps getting

better all the way along. It is this: the Master has
planned that your life journey shall be a personally
conducted one on this ideal plan. It was said a
night or two ago that the Master has thought into
your life and made arrangement for all its needs.
Let me add to-night this further fact: *He has
arranged with His best friend, who is an experienced traveler, to go with you and devote Himself
wholly to your interests.*

Some of you, I am afraid, will smile, and think
that I am just indulging in a fancy sketch—drawing on my imagination. And so I pray our Master
to burn into our hearts that it is plain, matter-of-
fact truth, for every day life. I would say that it is
cold fact were it not that such a fact can never
be cold.

POWER IS A PERSON

Each of these talks, you have noticed, has led up
to the one idea of surrender. That word surrender
stands for one side only of a transaction—*our* side.
As in all transactions, there is another side—*His*
side to whom the surrender is made. To-night we
want to take a step in advance and talk about the
part which Jesus has in this surrender-transaction.
All truth goes in pairs. The partnership word with
surrender is mastery. Surrender on my part is followed by mastery on His part. There are two per-
sonalities in this transaction. You are one: an
important one, but only one. To-night we shall try
to get a better acquaintance with the other One.
The One who assumes control of the surrendered
life, who is to be our personal guide and friend.

Will you recall again the Master's good-bye Olivet message, and notice just what it means? Listen to the very words: "Ye shall receive power." Let me ask you—what is power? Will some one give a simple definition of that word? There are four words, four of the commonest, most familiar in our language, for which I have not been able to find a definition. If some one here can help me I will be grateful. They are the words life, light, love, and power. What do they mean? I can find plenty of statements *about* them, descriptions of what each of these is like, but no definitions.

What is life? Recently I looked into the statement regarding life made by three of the most famous English scientists of the nineteenth century, whose names are household words. I read them carefully. The wisdom and keenness of observation they show are amazing. But when I had studied and read them repeatedly I found myself asking—what *is* life? They have described readily the functions and characteristics of life, but have not told what it is. They do not seem to know. Do you?

What is light? Will some one tell me? The corpuscular theory, which the famous Newton advocated, is long since abandoned. The later wave theory is pretty generally accepted, and yet they can not all agree upon that. These people say that light is a part of the kind of energy called radiant energy. Now, we all know what light is! The sun of course is not light, only a light-holder and distributer. According to the oldest record we have of the creation, light existed before these light-holders, the sun and moon and stars.

What is love? Well, you all *know,* I hope. Pity
the poor man who does not know by experience
what love is. But you cannot tell what it is. "Oh!"
you say, "it is emotion." Yes, so is hate, its very
opposite. "Well, love is affection." Yes. What is
affection? "Well, it is a pleasurable feeling, or
regard, which may be very intense, and which leads
us to unlimited sacrifice if need be. It is a devotion
that grips the soul tremendously." That is true;
yet that is only telling what love is like. No simple,
plain definition of love, or light or life has ever been
formed yet by man so far as I can learn.

What is power? You may say it is force. And
what is force? "Well, force is a form of energy."
What is energy? "Well," you reply, "it is a strong
inward movement whose strength is very impres-
sive." Some one says "power is ability." And ability?
"Well, that is the innate power to do something."
And so we get to use our word in the attempted
definition itself, which is simply talking in a circle.
We can find good descriptive words, but no defining
words.

Now mark a singular fact. In the writings of
John, in this old book I have here, you will find a
few statements regarding these things which com-
bine wondrous simplicity of language with marvelous, yes, unfathomable, depth of meaning. First,
about life: in chapter one, verse four, of the gospel:
—"in Him was life," being an evident allusion to
the remarkable Genesis statement: "the Lord God
breathed into his nostrils the breath of life, and
man became a living soul." Then, about love: in
chapter four, verse seven, of his first epistle:—
"love is of God"; coupled with the twice spoken

words "God is love" in the same chapter. About
light: in chapter one, verse five, of the same
epistle, "God is light."

I know some of you, perhaps some skilled theo-
logian here, is saying to himself, "Those are statements of *moral* truths." And I understand that
that is the common conception. But I want to state
here my own profound conviction, based on the
Spirit-breathed words of John, that some day, when
we shall know about all these deep things, we shall
be finding that there is a basis not only of moral
truth, but of far more than moral truth underlying
those profoundly simple statements.

And I believe in that day we shall find that life—
all life—is, in some actual, marvelous way, the out-
breathing of God's own being. And that light is
the inherent radiance of His person and face, and
that the universal passion of love is the throbbing
pulse-beat of His own great heart.

Now why take time to speak about these things
to-night when we are talking about power? I will
tell you why. Because they give the intensest practical significance to a similar statement about that
word power with which we *are* greatly concerned
just now.

Mark the language Luke uses in describing that
memorable Olivet scene in which we are so deeply
interested in these talks together. The old King
James version reads: "ye shall receive power *after*
that the Holy Spirit is come upon you." The
revised version puts it in this way, "ye shall receive
power *when* the Holy Spirit is come upon you."
Some of you have probably noticed that some edi-
tions give a marginal note, which, in this case,

proves to be the literal reading namely: *ye shall receive power the Holy Spirit coming upon you.* Not "after," nor "when," but simply "the Holy Spirit coming," etc. That is to say, *the Holy Spirit is power.* That you will observe fits in with the form of statement John uses. The Holy Spirit in control, unhindered, unhampered, means power manifest in the life. That is the profound truth of God's book. And as a bit of side evidence it is striking to observe that all Scripture statements throughout fit in with that conception. Power is a person. Not some thing, nor influence, nor sentiment, nor some working upon our hearts at a distance by God seated up yonder on the throne. That were wonderful indeed. But a person, called the Holy Spirit, living in me—shall I make it very definite by saying, living *in my body?*—that is power. If restrained by sin, or disobedience, or ignorance, or wilfulness of any sort, then power *restrained*, held in check, not evident. If utterly unrestrained, given free sway and control—ah! then power manifest, limitless, wonderful, all exercised in carrying out God's will in, and with, and through me.

And the marvelous message I bring you from the old Book of God is this: *The Master has sent a dear friend of His, and of yours, who is experienced, and strong, and loving, personally to conduct you through your daily life, and His presence unrestrained, means power unlimited.*

A SIGNIFICANT NAME

Do you remember that heart-to-heart talk that Jesus had with the eleven disciples that last night they spent together in the upper room? John tells us about it in chapters thirteen to sixteen. The Master talks a great deal that night, about some One else, who was coming to take His place with them. They did not understand what He meant till afterwards. He packs more into that one evening's talk about this coming One than all He had said before put together. Notice that now He gives a name, a new name, to this person, repeated four times that night. It is an intensely significant name —*the Comforter*. Will you remember, and keep constantly in mind, the actual meaning of that new name? it is simply this: *one called alongside to help*.

Let me attempt to suggest a little of its practical meaning.

Here is a little girl standing on the curbstone down town on Broadway in New York, with a bundle in her arms. She has been sent on an errand, and wants to get across the street. But the electric cars are whizzing past in both directions, and wagons, and carriages, and omnibuses, and horses jam the street from curb to curb, and she cannot get across. She stands there gripping her bundle, watching eagerly for a chance, and yet afraid to venture. But the jam seems endless, and she grows very tired, and by and by the corners of her mouth begin to twitch down suspiciously, and a big tear is just starting in each eye. Just then a big policeman steps up, one of the finest, six feet tall, and heavy and broad. He seems like a giant to her. He stoops down. Would you imagine he had such a gentle voice? "What's the matter?" "Can't— get—'cross." Oh! is that all; he'll fix that. And he takes her little hand in his with a reassuring "come along." And along she goes, past cars, under horses' heads, close up to big wheels. She is just as small as before, and just as weak. But though her eyes stay pretty big, the tears are gone, and there is an air of confidence, because this big, kind-hearted giant by her side is walking across the street as though he owned the whole place, *and he is devoting his entire attention to her.* That policeman is a comforter in the strict meaning of the word.

Here is a boy in school, head down close to the desk, puzzling over a "sum." It won't "come out." He figures away, and his brow is all knitted up, and a worried look is coming into his face for he is a conscientious little fellow. But he cannot seem to get it right and the clouds gather thicker. By and by the teacher comes up and sits down by his side. It awes him a little to have her quite so close. But her kindliness of manner mellows the awe. "How are you getting along?" "Won't come out right"—in a very despondent tone. "Let me see, did you subtract that . . . ?" "Oh-h-h! I forgot that," and a little light seems to break, as he scratches away for a few moments; then pauses. "And this figure here, should it be. . . ." "Oh-h-h, I see." More scratching, and a soft sigh of relief, and the knitting brows unravel, and the face brightens. The teacher did not do the problem for him. She did better. She let him feel her kindly interest first of all, and gave just the light, experienced touch that showed him the way out, and yet allowed him the peculiar pleasure of getting through himself. *That is what "Comforter" means.*

One summer a friend suggested to me spending

a week on Lake Chautauqua. I did not have the money to spare, and so told him I was not sure I could arrange to get away. But he seemed to divine the basis of my objection, and insisted on my going along. We went. I had very little money with me. I got on the train without a ticket. took a seat in the parlor car, stopped at the best hotel, had a choice room on the ground floor, patronized the well-ordered dining-room regularly, and made free use of the place. And all the time I had practically no money with me. But would you believe me I was not a particle concerned about paying for those privileges. Never felt less concern about anything in my life. You know why. *I had a trustworthy friend with me who was concerned for me.*

Now these are simple suggestions, illustrating *partly* the meaning of that marvelous name Jesus gave to the Holy Spirit. I will send another Comforter, one who will be right by your side to help, sympathetic, experienced, strong; and He will stay with you all the time. In the kitchen, in the sitting-room, the sick-room, with the children, when work piles up, when things jangle or threaten to, when the baby's cross, and the patching and sweeping and baking. and all the rest of it seem endless, on the street, in the office, on the campus, in the store, when tempted—almost slipped, when opportunity opens for a quiet personal word, everywhere, every time, in every circumstance, one alongside to help. Is not that wonderful?

A PICTORIAL ILLUSTRATION

There is one bother about illustrations: they

never do tell all the truth. They never are as vivid, not as good as the truth, that is when you are talking about our Master, or His arrangements. The very best illustrations of Bible truth are Bible illustrations. Now there is a striking pictorial illustration back in the Old Testament of the meaning of this name of the Holy Spirit. It is in the story of a most remarkable journey from Egypt to the border line of Palestine. The journey was remarkable for two things. First, for the sort of country it was through. It is a trackless waste of sand, that spreads over thousands of square miles. It was infested with venomous serpents and scorpions, and is described as "all that great and terrible wilderness," "a waste howling wilderness," and "a land of deserts and pits, of drought and of the shadow of death, that none passed through, and where no man dwelt." Think of taking a trip through a country like that! But it was even more remarkable because of the transformation that took place in the travelers. For a mob of four millions of people was changed into a well-organized nation. The explanation given is fully as remarkable as the trip, and the transformation. It must strike very strangely on the cold, matter-of-fact ears of this materialistic world we dwell in. It is this: that the Lord God Himself actually went with them in person, and lived with them, and took immediate charge of everything. He had promised Moses, their leader, that He would do this. Just how definite or indefinite a thing that meant to Moses' mind we cannot know. But it became very definite and tangible that memorable night of departure from the iron furnace of Egypt. For there was a real physical evidence of His presence. There appeared a column or pillar of fleecy-like cloud which came down close to the ground, and which every one could plainly see. At night time it shone and flamed as a pillar full of partly concealed fire. God's voice spake out of it in their hearing. And that presence-cloud never left them. In spite of complaints, and criticisms, and rebellions of the most mean and exasperating kind, it never left them until they had safely arrived at the border line of the promised Palestine.

Now it is extremely fascinating in tracing that journey to notice just what that cloud came to mean to them. If you will run rapidly through the three wilderness books, Exodus, Leviticus and Numbers, you will find there twenty distinct incidents [1] which illustrate how God's actual presence in that cloud was made very real to them in practical affairs. In those incidents there are ten different ways in which they were made to feel that powerful Presence.

At the outset it is mentioned that the chief purpose was "to lead them the way," and, by night "to give them light." Five incidents speak of bodily nourishment, including fresh food daily, with occasional extras, and a full supply of pure living water. Five speak of protection from bodily harm. Two tell of the defeat of an enemy. Once there is chiding for ingratitude. Six times rebuke or punishment for sin. In four they are held back when dead-set on a very wrong course. Twice there is instruction in their leader's plan for them. Three times a fuller manifestation of Himself, and each time this

[1] See note at the end.

is preceded by obedience on their part in some
particular matter. Once there is a special plan suggested for relief in managing the nation's affairs.
And then the fact is stated that whenever Moses
went apart to talk with God the cloud descended
lower, that is, *God came nearer* when Moses
desired to talk with Him. So you see, the cloud
meant guidance through that trackless desert, food
supplies, protection, defeat for the enemy, chiding,
restraint, punishment, instruction, help in business
matters, a more intimate manifestation of the
glorious personality of their Guide, and a gracious
coming nearer whenever desired. Was not that a
real practical presence of the great God with them
all those days?

Now that is the Bible's own graphic illustration
of the meaning of that new name given to the Holy
Spirit, by Him who knew Him best, *Comforter—
one alongside to help.*

On a Higher Level

Before we leave that illustration we must notice
a very significant thing which is no small part of
the truth illustrated. Though the cloud appeared
the very night of that sudden going out of Egypt,
and was never absent from them, by day or by
night, yet a full year afterwards there was a new
experience. By God's direction a special tent was
made and set up in which He said He would dwell.
It was known as God's dwelling place, the tent of
meeting, the tabernacle, the tent of testimony.
When everything concerning its setting up had
been fully done as specified then there was an

experience the most remarkable they had yet had
with God. It was a new manifestation of the glorious presence of their unseen Friend-Guide. It is
twice said that the tent was *"filled"* with His glory.
And this nearer disclosure, which God gave of Himself, was so marvelously glorious and overpowering
that even Moses, who had spent almost twelve
weeks in that mount with God, in closer intimacy
than any one else—even Moses was not able to
enter into the tent, so over-awing was that
Presence.

Now it is of intensest interest to mark four things
about that experience. *First* of all, before it came,
there was *obedience* to God's instructions. Eighteen
times within the narrow limits of the last two pages
of the Exodus record, it is said that Moses and the
people did everything, in every particular, just
exactly as "the Lord commanded Moses." There
was explicit obedience before anything else. *Then*
followed the wondrous *infilling* of the tent with
God's presence. The *third* thing is particularized
very carefully: all their movements were directed
and controlled by that Presence. Clearly the only
safe rule for living in that terrible desert, was to
plan to live a planless life so far as their own planning was concerned. Besides the last two verses of
Exodus which emphasize this, I find that in my
revised Oxford edition forty-five lines in the ninth
chapter of Numbers are given to telling how
exactly they were guided, and how explicitly they
followed their Guide. It seems almost at first reading as though there was a decidedly needless repetition. You seem to understand the thing easily
enough without that. But as one reads it again, and

yet again, slowly, it begins to dawn upon the mind
that the purpose is to put marked emphasis on this
feature of their new life in the wilderness. The
people would rise in the morning, and probably
the first thing done was to look out toward the
cloud to learn if there was to be any change that
day. And so during the day there would come to be
an instinctive habit of watching that cloud. They
might remain in a new camping place for months,
or only for a few weeks, or, possibly only for a few
days. They never knew a day ahead. They lived
literally a day at a time. It was certainly a hand-to-
mouth existence so far as the daily manna was
concerned. But then it was from *His* hand to *their*
mouths and that made a great difference. It was
equally so in their movements and in all of their
new life. When, one morning as thousands of
heads peep out, the cloud is seen to have lifted up
from over the tent, the next question was—which
direction? It might be toward the west, or it might
be just the opposite, toward the east. Both the time
of going, and the direction, and the pace were
regulated by the presence of their Friend in that
cloud. Their life was a life of obedience to the will
of their wise, loving Companion.

The *fourth* thing was intimacy of intercourse. It
is a little unfortunate that in reading our Bibles we
sometimes allow the gaps that come in the printing
to break the continuity of thought. There is a break
for instance between the last verse of Exodus and
the first verse of Leviticus. The reading is meant
to be continuous, and shows that after the infilling,
and the explanation about guidance, that God

"called" Moses to Him and *commenced talking about their new life.* Now in connection with that call, and all their after talks, notice a remarkable statement in the last verse of that long seventh chapter of Numbers. It explains just *how* God talked with Moses. Listen: "Whenever Moses went into the tent of meeting to speak with Him, *then he heard the voice* speaking unto him from above the mercy-seat that was upon the ark of the testimony, from between the two cherubim; and *He* speaketh unto him." There was the living, loving voice of their Companion-God, which Moses could plainly hear, and which others heard, talking familiarly and intimately about all their affairs. Several times when in doubt what to do Moses promptly went off into the tent, then the cloud would come down nearer, and Moses would state his difficulty, and back would come that clear distinct voice with an answer. Group up those four things—obedience; the never-to-be-forgotten infilling; the controlling guidance; and intimate companionship.

That is the very best illustration I can find of the meaning of that word which Jesus now chooses out and uses as the new name which would most vividly tell what the Holy Spirit was to be all believers after His own departure. All that the presence of God in that pillar was to those people, and to Moses personally, all that the Holy Spirit will be to you. And my own conviction is that Jesus had that Old Testament scene in His mind. For if you will turn again to that last night's talk you will find a striking repetition of the steps or peculiarities of that wilderness experience. Though here the whole experience is on a much higher, finer plane. There is a closeness of personal regard, a depth of that deepest of all loves, friendship love, that is not found in the Old Testament story, except perhaps between Moses himself and God.

But now read the twenty-first verse of the fourteenth chapter of John: "He that hath My commandments and keepeth them, he it is that loveth Me; and he that loveth Me shall be loved of My Father, and I will love him, and *will manifest Myself unto him.*" And the twenty-third verse adds to it: "If a man love Me, he will keep My word: and My Father will love him, and *We will come unto him and make Our abiding place with him.*" Notice: there is obedience; it is accepted as an evidence of love: there is a return love—a new, higher, reciprocal love: then there is a revealing of Himself; and, constant abiding. Now run your eye through the remaining part of that evening's conversation and you can quickly pick out these words: "teach," "bring to your remembrance," "guide," "bear witness of me," "tell you coming things," "tell you about me."

Does that not parellel remarkably the wilderness experience? Only it is all put on such a higher plane. There is a fullness, and richness, and tenderness, of personal intimacy here. The Presence in the wilderness was for the national life: here it is peculiarly for the personal life. There He dwelt actually in the heart of the nation. Here He dwells actually in one's own very person. And then, too, now He can do so much more *in* us because so much more has been done for us through the person of Jesus.

How to Find the Meaning

May I say right here plainly: there seems to be even yet in some quarters a hazy idea about the Holy Spirit being a person. It is extremely common, even among people of excellent christian training, to find Him referred to, both in prayer and speech as *it*. Could anything be more disrespectful or insulting, if it were intentional instead of being thoughtless or, in ignorance, as I am sure it really is. Imagine my speaking of the pastor of this church in that way. "*It* is a good preacher. *It* is a helpful pastor." You smile, and he smiles. But if I said it repeatedly, and in sober earnest, you know how insulted he would be. I suppose that the use of the word "itself" for the Holy Spirit in the eighth chapter of Romans is largely responsible for this. The revisers have properly substituted the word "himself." That very usage so common has doubtless accustomed many persons to a vague idea of the personality of the Spirit. And yet apart from that, there is without doubt much mistiness, and uncertainty, in some minds, because of the difficulty of thinking of a person without a form. It seems impossible for our minds to grasp the idea of existence without bodily shape, yet of course we believe in a personal God. Probably another reason is that the Holy Spirit's work is not to speak of Himself but of Another—of Jesus. He is Jesus' representative, and is constantly absorbed in filling us with thoughts of His Chief. And when our minds are most deeply stirred with thoughts of Jesus then it is that in that very fact of being so

stirred we have clearest evidence of the Holy
Spirit's presence within us. His very faithfulness to
His mission has led to Himself suffering deprecia-
tion at our hands, through our ignorance.

I am sure it must help us all decidedly in getting
a clear-cut, sharply defined idea of His personality
to notice the language Jesus uses in speaking of
Him that night. For instance, notice that in our
English version the personal pronouns "he,"
"whom," "him," "which" (used in the sense of who
as is common with the British translators), occur
twenty-four times. A study of the actual words used
would prove helpful and interesting. One of them,
used several times, is peculiarly emphatic, its
meaning being equivalent to the expression "that
person there."

And then notice the words used to describe what
this person will do: "He shall teach," "bring to
your remembrance," "bear witness of Me," "convict the world of" three distinct things, "shall guide,"
"shall hear," "shall speak," "shall declare," "shall
glorify Me," "shall take of Mine and declare it unto
you." Everyone of these ten different expressions
imply intelligence and discrimination, and therefore of course personality. And then added to this
is the name given to Him here of which so much
has been said.

May we take just another look at that name—
The Comforter—as we close our talk together? I
wish with my whole heart, and I pray, that a vivid
sense of the meaning of that name may be one
result of this evening's meeting. I was traveling
alone in Germany one hot July day on a train going
down to the city of Worms. It was quite hot and I

was very tired, and my head aching, I distinctly remember. The conductor came along and objected to my ticket. Before leaving this country, I thought I knew a *little* of German, enough to worry through on. My ideas on that subject changed a trifle over there, however. That day my tired ears refused to recognize any familiar sounds on the conductor's lips, and my tired tongue refused to utter anything satisfactory to him. And there I was, a complete stranger in a strange land too tired to think or have any mental resources, not knowing but I might be put off at the next station. In fact just tired enough for fine worrying. It looked blue for a few moments. But not for long. A young man by my side, a Jew, spoke to me in excellent English. Was any sound ever so welcome! He straightened the conductor out, and then we fell to talking together. He proved to be a very intelligent, agreeable companion. I found his home was in the city where I was going. So we got off there together, and he simply devoted himself to me for the day. He took me up to a good hotel, and while I was eating dinner, went and got his brother who had been in America, and who entertained me while I ate. Then he took me to his father's home, a large old mansion, overlooking the famous Luther monument, where I rested a while. And then a quick run to a few interesting points, and finally when leaving time came, he insisted on accompanying me to the station, and making sure I had a good seat, and then bade me a gracious good-bye.

That day lingers in my memory as one of the green spots of that trip. It touched me to think that my Master graciously sent one of His own despised race to be my friend. Do you not think that that man, experienced where I was ignorant, and so sympathetic, was a living illustration to me of Jesus' name for the Holy Spirit—*one called alongside to help*?

One day recently, riding on a Lake Shore train in Ohio, I chanced to notice the conductor stopping to speak to a little girl sitting behind me. Then I noticed that she was alone and crying a little, quietly. She did not answer his questions, but he must have been a father, I thought, because he seemed to understand so well. Speaking to a kind-faced motherly looking woman in the next seat he had the little girl go back and sit beside her, next the window. They did not talk much, if any, I noticed. But the girl was snuggled up close, and I knew from her face that she felt the warm sympathy of that friendly presence, and that the terrible feeling of loneliness had gone. Is not that woman another illustration of that name Comforter? Her mere presence was all that was needed to clear the skies and change the atmosphere for the little lone and lonely traveler.

But Jesus Himself has a very striking way of making clear just what He meant, by coupling another word with that new name the first time He used it. He says, "I will send *another* Comforter." The comparison is with Himself. He is one comforter. The Holy Spirit another one. The only other time this word is used is by John in his first epistle, and is translated by our word advocate, and refers to Jesus. Jesus practically says: "You know what I have been to you these months past." And they would think through the close intimacy of nearly two years. How He had spoken with unmistakable plainness when they were in the wrong, but also how loving with a strong love He had been, how patient, and gentle, and resourceful, and how He seemed to yearn over them that they might grow into His ideal for them. "Now," He says, "I am going away, but I will send you *another* one who will be to you all that I have been—*and more.*" *And more!* That comparative more, either spoken or implied, runs all through this last long confidential talk. "More, much more, *because I go unto the Father.*" Jesus crucified, risen, glorified can do much more by far in us by His other self, the Holy Spirit, than He could in person on the earth those years. And the wondrous meaning of that "another comforter" to you and me, my friends, to-night is simply this: it is the same as though the Lord Jesus had actually come back again and *you had Him all to yourself—and more.*

But I cannot tell you the meaning of that wonderful name. Nor yet the wondrous charm of Him, who, for our sakes, embodies it. You may put together all these illustrations in the attempt to get a real, close-up, idea of what Jesus meant in that love-gift of His to you. And then you will not know. There is really only one way to gain that knowledge. It is this: take the step which belongs to *your* side of the transaction between you and the Master. Surrender yourself to Him to be changed and cleansed and used as He may choose. Then *He* will begin at once working out the side that belongs to Him. *You shall be filled with His presence.* Then you will *begin* to know. Then you can sing—

I have a wonderful guest,
   Who speeds my feet, who moves my hands,
   Who strengthens, comforts, guides, commands,
Whose presence gives me rest.

He dwells within my soul,
   He swept away the filth and gloom;
   He garnished fair the empty room,
And now pervades the whole.

And you shall go on knowing more and better until the day dawn and the shadows flee away.

Of the twenty incidents referred to three do not directly mention the cloud, and in two others it is over the mount, with its characteristics much intensified. The references are given for those who will want to get closer up to this famous illustration.

Guidance: Ex. xiii:21–22, with Numbers xiv:14.

Bodily nourishment: Ex. xv:25; xvi:13–14, 45; xvii:6. Numbers xi:31–32. xx:1–12.

Protection from bodily harm: The nation—Ex. xiv:19–20. The leaders—Num. xiv:10 and on. xvi:19 and on. xvi:42 and on. xx:1–12.

Defeat of an enemy: Ex. xiv:24–31; xvii:8–16.

Chiding: Ex. xvi:4–7, 10–12.

Rebuke or punishment for sin: Numbers xi:33; xii:1–10; xiv:10 and on; xvi:19 and on; 42 and on; xx:1–12.

Held back from wrong: Numbers xiv:10 and on; xvi:19 and on; 42 and on; xx:1–12.

Instruction and training: Ex. xix:9, 16 and on; xxiv:15–18.

Fuller manifestation: Ex. xxxiv:5 and on; xl:34–38. Lev. ix:6, 23.

Special plan of relief in management: Numbers xi:16, 17, 25.

Coming nearer: Ex. xxxiii:7–11, revised version.

Making and Breaking Connections

MANY EXPERIENCES, BUT ONE LAW

In mechanics power depends on good connections. A visit to any great machine shop makes that clear. There must be good connections in two directions —inward toward the source of power, and outward for use. The same law holds true in spiritual power as in mechanical. There must be good connections.

These nights we have been together a few things have seemed clear. We have seen that from the standpoint of our lives there is *need* of power, as well as from the standpoint of the Master's use of us among others. Jesus' promise and insistent words make plain the *necessity* of our having power if His plan for us is not to fail. His words about the *price* of power have set many of us to doing some honest thinking and heart-searching. And we have gotten some suggestion, too, of the meaning of that word power, and of the *personality* back of the word.

To-night I want to talk with you a little about
how to secure good connections between the source
of power and the channel through which it is to
flow out to others; and, once secured, how to
preserve the connections unbroken.

It has been one of the peculiar characteristics of
recent years in religious circles that much has been
spoken and written about the Holy Spirit. Thousands of persons have been led into a clearer understanding of His personality and mission, and
into intimate relationship with Himself. And yet,
may I say frankly, that I read much and listened
to much without being able to get a simple work-
able understanding of how I was to receive the
much-talked-of baptism of power. That may quite
likely have been due to my own dullness of com-
prehension. But whatever the cause, my failing to
understand led to a rather careful study of the old
Book itself until somewhat clearer light has come.
And now in this convention I am anxious to put
the truth as simply as I may that others may not
blunder and bungle along and lose precious time
as I have done.

Many an earnest heart, conscious of weakness
and failure, is asking, how may I have power to
resist temptation, and live a strong, useful, christian life? In the search for an answer some of us
have run across two difficulties. One of these is in
other people's experiences. It is very natural to try
to find out how someone else has succeeded in
getting what we are after. Many a godly man has
told of his experience of waiting and pleading with
God before the thing he sought came. Personal
experiences are intensely interesting, and often

helpful. But there are apt to be as many different sorts of experiences as there are persons. Yet there is one unchanging law of God's dealing with men underlying them all. But unless one is more skilled than many of us are in analyzing experiences and discovering the underlying law, these experiences of others are often misleading. We are so likely to think at once of the desirability of having the same experience as someone else, rather than trying to find God's law of spirit life in them all. And so, some of the written experiences have clouded rather than cleared the sky. We should rather try *first* to get something of a clear understanding of God's law of dealing with men as a sort of basis to build upon. And then fit into that, even though it may develop differently in our circumstances. We may then get much help from others' experiences. If possible, we want to-night to get something of an inkling of that law.

Another difficulty that has bothered some of us is in the great variety of language used in speaking of this life of power; a variety that seems confusing to some of us. "The baptism of the Holy Spirit," "the induement," "the filling," "refilling," "many fillings," "special anointings"—these terms are familiar, though just the distinctive meaning of each is not always clear. Let us look a little at the language of the Book at this point. A run through the New Testament brings out five leading words used in speaking of the Holy Spirit's relation to us. These words are "baptized," "filled," "anointed," "sealed," and "earnest." It seems to take all five words to tell all of the truth. Each gives a different side.

The word *baptized* is the distinctive word always used *before* the day of Pentecost, in speaking of what was to occur then. It is not used afterward except in referring back to that day. It belongs peculiarly to the day of Pentecost. Each of the gospels tells that John the Baptist said that Jesus was to baptize with the Holy Spirit. Jesus Himself uses the word, during the forty days, in Acts first chapter. Peter, in Acts, eleventh chapter, recalls this remark. Paul uses it once in referring back to Pentecost.[1] These seem to be the only instances where the word is used in speaking of the Holy Spirit. One other word is used once in advance of Pentecost. "Tarry until ye be *endued* or clothed upon." [2] We shall see in a few moments that the meaning of this fits in with the meaning of baptized, emphasizing one part of its meaning.

"Baptized" may be called the *historical* word. It describes an act done once for all on that great day of Pentecost, with possibly four accessory repetitions to make clear that additional classes and groups were included.[3] It tells God's side.

In this connection it will be helpful to note the significance of the word baptize. Of course you

[1] 1 Cor. xii: 13.

[2] Luke xxiv: 49.

[3] That is to make perfectly plain that this experience was for *all:* a very difficult fact for these intensely Jewish disciples to grasp.

(1) Not limited to the original one hundred and twenty, but for the whole body of Jewish disciples—Acts iv.

(2) For the hated half-breed Samaritans—Acts viii.

(3) For the "dogs" of Gentiles—Acts x.

(4) For individual disciples anywhere, and at any distance in time from Pentecost—Acts xix.

will understand that I am not speaking now of the matter or mode of water baptism. But I am supposing that originally or historically the word means a plunging or dipping into. We commonly think of the act of immersion-baptism from the side of the object immersed because the action is on the side of the thing or person which is plunged down into the immersing flood. But in the historical baptism of the Holy Spirit at Pentecost the standpoint is reversed. Instead of a plunging down into there is a coming down upon, exactly reversing the order with which we are familiar, but with the same result—submersion. Notice the phrases in Acts used in describing the baptism of the Holy Spirit on that historical Pentecost: "Coming upon you," "pour out," "poured forth," "fallen upon," "fell upon," "poured out," "fell on them," "came upon," [1] all suggesting an act from above.

A Four-Sided Truth

Now notice that the word used at the time of the actual occurrence and afterwards is another word —"*filled*" and "full," which occurs eleven times in the first nine chapters of Acts. It tells what was *experienced* by those persons at Pentecost and afterwards. It describes *their* side. Baptism was the *act;* filling was the *result.* If you plunge a book into water you are submerging the book: that is your side. The leaves of the book quickly become soaked, filled with the water: that is the other side. When a baby is born it is plunged out into the atmosphere. That is an immersion into air. It

[1] Acts i:8; ii:17, 33; viii:15; x:45; xix:6.

begins at once to cry and its lungs become filled with the air into which it has been plunged. So here "filled" is the *experience* word; it tells our side.

The third word, *"anointed,"* indicates the *purpose* of this filling; it is to qualify for living and for service. It is the word commonly used in the Old Testament for the setting apart of the tabernacle to its holy use; and of priests and kings, and sometimes prophets for service and leadership. In the New Testament it is four times used of Jesus, each time in connection with His public ministry.[1] Paul uses it of himself in answering those who had criticised his work and leadership at Corinth.[2] And John uses it twice in speaking of ability to discern and teach the truth.[3] It is the *power* word, indicating that the Holy Spirit's coming is for the specific purpose of setting us apart, and to qualify us for right living, and for acceptable and helpful service.

The fourth word, *"sealed,"* explains our personal connection with the Lord Jesus. It is used once by Paul in writing to his friends at Corinth, and twice in the Ephesian epistle.[4] The seal was used, and still is to mark ownership. In our lumber regions up in the Northwest it is customary to clear a small spot on a log and strike it with the blunt end of a hatchet containing the initials of the owner, and then send it adrift down the stream with hundreds

[1] (1) Luke iv:18, quo. from Isa. lxi:1. (2) Acts iv:27. (3) Acts x:38. (4) Heb. i:9, quotation from Ps. xlv:7.
[2] 2 Cor. i:21.
[3] 1 John i:20, 27.
[4] 2 Cor. i:22. Eph. i:13; iv:30.

of others, and though it may float miles unguarded, that mark of ownership is respected. On the Western plains it is common to see mules with an initial branded on the flank. In both cases the initial is the owner's seal, recognized by law as sufficient evidence of ownership. So the Holy Spirit is Jesus' ownership mark stamped upon us to indicate that we belong to Him. He is our sole Owner. And if any of us are not allowing Him to have full control of His property, we are dealing dishonestly. Sealed is the *property* or *ownership* word.

The last one of these words, *"earnest,"* is a peculiarly interesting one. It is found three times in Paul's epistles.[1] An earnest is a pledge given in advance as an evidence of good faith. We are familiar with the usage of paying down a small part of the price agreed upon to make a business transaction binding. In old English it is called caution money. My mother has told me of seeing her mother many a time pay a shilling in the Belfast market-house to insure the delivery of a bag of potatoes, paying the remainder on its delivery.

Now here the Holy Spirit is called "the earnest of our inheritance unto the redemption of the purchased possession." That means two things to us: First—that the Holy Spirit now filling us is Jesus' pledge that He has purchased us, and that some day He is coming back to claim His possessions; and then that the measure of the Spirit's presence and power now is only a foretaste of a greater fullness at the time of coming back; a sort of partial advance payment which insures a payment

[1] 2 Cor. i:22; v:5. Eph. i:14.

in full when the transaction is completed. Paul speaks of this to the Romans as the *first fruits* of the Spirit.[1]

So, if you will take all five words you will get all of the truth about our friend the Holy Spirit, and just what His coming into one's life means. The first word, "baptism," is the *historical* word, pointing us *back* to the day of Pentecost. The other four words, taken together, tell us the four sides of the Holy Spirit's relation to us now. "Filled" is the *experience* word, pointing us *inward* to what actually takes place there. "Anointed" is the *power* word, pointing us *outward* to the life and service among men to which we are set apart. "Sealed" is the *personal-relation* word, pointing us *upward* to our Owner and Master. "Earnest" is the *prophetic* word, pointing us *forward* to the Master's coming back to claim His own, and to bestow the full measure of the Spirit's presence.

And to-night we want to get some hint of how to have this infilling, which shall also be an anointing of power and a seal of ownership and an earnest of greater things at Jesus' return.

BROKEN COUPLINGS

But perhaps some one is saying, "Have not we all received the Holy Spirit if we are christians?" Yes, that is quite true. It is the Holy Spirit's presence in us that makes us christians. His work begins at conversion. Conversion and regeneration are the two sides of the same transaction. Con-

[1] Romans viii:23.

version, the human side: regeneration, the divine side. My turning clear around to God is my side, and instantly His Spirit enters and begins His work. But here is a distinction to be made: the Holy Spirit is in every christian, but in many He is not allowed free and full control, and so there is little or none of His power *felt* or *seen*. Only as He has full sway is His power *manifest*. If at the time of conversion or decision there is clear instruction and a wholehearted surrender, there will be evidence of the Spirit's presence at once. And if the new life goes on *without break* there will be a continuance of that power in ever-increasing measure. But many a time, through ignorance, or through some disobedience or failure to obey, there has come a break, a slipping of a cog somewhere, and so an interruption of the flow of power. Many a time lack of instruction regarding the cultivation of the Spirit's friendship has resulted in just such a break. And so a new start is necessary. Then a full surrender is followed by a new experience or, shall I better say, a re-experience of the Spirit's presence. And this new experience sometimes is so sharply marked as to begin a new epoch in the life. Some of the notable leaders of the Church have gone through just such an experience.

Yet, I know a man—have known him somewhat intimately for years—one of the most saintly men it has been my privilege to know. For some years he was a missionary abroad, but now is preaching in this country. His private personal life is fragrant, and his public speech is always accompanied with rare power. In conversation with a young minister at a summer conference, he said he had never

known his second blessing or experience on which
such stress was being laid there. And I think I can
readily understand that he had not. For, apparently, so far as one can see, his first surrender or
decision had been a whole-hearted one. He had
followed simply, fully, as he saw the way. There
had been no break, but a steady going on and up,
and an ever-increasing manifestation of the Spirit's
presence from the time of that first decision. So
that it may be said, quite accurately, I think, that
in God's plan there is no need of any second stage,
but *in our actual experience* there has been a
second stage, and sometimes more than a second,
too, because with so many of us the connections
have been broken, making a fresh act on our part
a necessity.

THE REAL BATTLEFIELD

But now the main topic we are to talk about is
making and breaking connections. First, making
connections with the source of power. How may
one who has been willing to go thus far in these
talks go a step further and have power in actual
conscious possession?

There are many passages in this old Book that
answer that question. But let me turn you to one
which puts the answer in very simple shape. John's
gospel, seventh chapter, verses thirty-seven to
thirty-nine. Listen: "Now, on the last day, the
great day of the feast, Jesus stood and cried, saying, if any man thirst, let him come unto me and
drink. He that believeth on me, as the Scripture
hath said, out of his belly shall flow rivers of living

water." Then John, writing some fifty years or so afterwards, adds what he himself did not understand at the time: "But this spake He of the Spirit who they that believed on Him were to receive; for not yet was the Spirit given, because not yet was Jesus glorified."

There are four words here which tell the four steps into a new life of power. Sometimes these steps are taken so quickly that they seem in actual experience like only one. But that does not matter to us just now, for we are after the practical result. Four words—thirst, glorified, drink, believe—tell the whole story. Thirst means desire, intense desire. There is no word in our language so strong to express desire as the word thirst. Physical thirst will completely control your actions. If you are very thirsty, you can do nothing till that gnawing desire is satisfied. You cannot read, nor study, nor talk, nor transact business. You are in agony when intensely thirsty. To die of thirst is extremely painful. Jesus uses that word thirst to express intensest desire. Let me ask you—Are you thirsty for power? Is there a yearning down in your heart for something you have not? That is the first step. No good to offer food to a man without appetite. "Blessed are they that hunger and thirst." Pitiable are they that need and do not know their need. Physicians find their most difficult work in dealing with the man who has no desire to live. He is at the lowest ebb. Are you thirsty? There is a special promise for thirsty ones. "I will pour water on him that is thirsty." If you are not thirsty for the Master's power, are you thirsty to be made thirsty? If you are not really thirsty in your heart for this

new life of power, you might ask the Master to put
that thirst in you. For there can be nothing before
that.

The second word is the one added long afterwards by John, when the Spirit had enlightened his
understanding—"glorified." "For not yet was the
Spirit given, because not yet was Jesus glorified."
That word has two meanings here: the first meaning a historical one, the second a personal or ex-
perimental one. The historical meaning is this:
when Jesus returned home all scarred in face and
form from His trip to earth, He was received back
with great enthusiasm, and was glorified in the
presence of myriads of angel beings by being en-
throned at the Father's right hand. Then the glorified Jesus sent the Holy Spirit down to the earth as
His own personal representative for His new peculiar mission. The presence of the Spirit in our hearts
is evidence that the Jesus whom earth despised and
crucified is now held in highest honor and glory
in that upper world. The Spirit is the gift of a
glorified Jesus. Peter lays particular stress upon this
in his Pentecost sermon, telling to those who had so
spitefully murdered Jesus that He "being at the
right hand of God *exalted* . . . hath poured forth
this." That is the historical meaning—the first
meaning—of that word "glorified." It refers to an
event in the highest heaven after Jesus' ascension.
The *personal* meaning is this: when Jesus is en-
throned in my life the Holy Spirit shall fill me. The
Father glorified Jesus by enthroning Him. I must
glorify Him by enthroning Him. But the throne of
my heart was occupied by another who did not pro-

pose to resign, nor to be deposed without resistance. So there had to be a dethronement as well as an enthronement. I must quietly but resolutely place the crown of my life, my love, my *will* upon Jesus' brow for Him henceforth to control me as He will. That act of enthroning Him carries with it the dethronement of self.

Let me say plainly that here is *the* searching test of the whole matter. *Why* do you want power? For the rare enjoyment of ecstatic moods? For some hidden selfish purpose, like Simon of Samaria, of which you are perhaps only half conscious, so subtly does it lurk underneath? That you may be able to move men? These motives are all selfish. The streams turn in, and that means a dead sea. Better stop before you begin. For thy heart is not right before God. But if the uppermost and undermost desire be to glorify Jesus and let Him do in you, and with you *what He chooses*, then you shall know the flooding of the channel-ways of your life with a new stream of power.

Jesus Himself, when down here as Son of Man, met this test. With reverence be it said that His highest purpose in coming to earth was not to die upon the cross, but to glorify His Father. That memorable passage opening the sixty-first chapter of Isaiah, which Jesus applied to Himself in the Nazareth synagogue, contains eight or nine statements of what He was to do, but closes with a comprehensive statement of the underlying purpose— *"that He might be glorified."* As it turned out, that could best be done by yielding to the awful experiences through which He passed. But the supreme thought of pleasing His Father was never absent from His thought. It drove Him to the wilderness, and to Gethsemane, and to Calvary.

Is that the one purpose in your heart in desiring power? He might send some of us out to the far-off foreign mission field. He might send some down to the less enchanted field of the city slums to do salvage service night after night among the awful social wreckage thrown upon the strand there; or possibly it would mean an isolated post out on the frontier, or down in the equally heroic field of the mountains of the South. He might leave some of you just where you are, in a commonplace, hum-drum spot, as you think, when your visions had been in other fields. He might make you a seed-sower, like lonely Morrison in China, when *you* wanted to be a harvester like Moody. Here is the real battlefield. The fighting and agonizing are here. Not with God but with yourself, that the old self in you may be crucified and Jesus crowned in its place.

Will you *in the purpose of your heart* make Jesus absolute monarch whatever that may prove to mean? It *may* mean great sacrifice; it *will* mean greater joy and power at once. May we have the simple courage to do it. Master, help us! Thou wilt help us. Thou art helping some of us now as we talk and listen and think.

Power Manifest in Action

Well, then, if you have won on that field of action, the rest is very simple. Indeed, after a victory there, your whole life moves up to a new

level. The third word is drink. "Let him come
unto Me *and drink.* Drinking is one of the easiest
acts imaginable. I wish I had a glass of water here
just to let you see how easy a thing it is. Tip up
the glass and let the water run in and down. Drink
simply means *take.* It is saying, "Lord Jesus, I
take from Thee the promised power. . . . I thank
Thee that the Spirit has taken full control." But
you say, "It that all?" Yes. "Why, I do not feel
anything." Do you remember saying something
like that when you were urged to take Jesus as
your Savior? And some kind friend told you not
to wait for feeling, but to trust, and that when you
did that, the light came? Now, the fourth word is
believe. The law of God's dealing with you has not
changed. Jesus says, "Out of his belly *shall flow*
rivers of living water." You are to believe His
word. "But," you say, "how shall I *know* I have
this power?" Well, first, by *believing* that Jesus
has done what He agreed. He promised the Spirit
to them that obey Him. The Holy Spirit fills every
surrendered heart. Then there is a second way—
you will experience the power as need arises. How
do you know *anything?* Here is this chair. Suppose I tell you I have power to pick it up and hold
it out at arm's length. Well, you think, I look as
though I might have that much power in my arm.
But you do not know. Perhaps my arm is weak
and does not show it. But now I pick it up and hold
it out—(holding chair out at arm's length)—now
you *know* I have at least that much power in my
arm. Power is always manifest in action. That is a
law of power. How did that man by the pool of
Bethesda in Jerusalem, who had not walked for

thirty-eight years—how did he *know* that he had received power to walk? *He got up and walked!* He did not know he had received the power till he got up. Power is shown in action always. Faith acts. It pushes out, in obedience to command. And when you go out of here to-day, *as the need arises* you will find the power rising within you to meet it. When the hasty word comes hot to your lips, when the old habit asserts itself, when the actual test of sacrifice comes, when the opportunity for service comes, as surely as the need comes, will come the sense of *His power* in control. Believe means *expect.*

"Thirst," "glorify," "drink," "believe"—*desire, enthrone, accept, expect*—that is the simple story. Are you thirsty? Will you put Jesus on the throne? Then accept, and go out with your eyes open, expecting, expecting, *expecting,* and He will never fail to reveal His power. Shall we bow in silence a few moments and settle the matter, each of us, with the Master direct?

Three Laws of Continuous Power

Power depends on good connections. In mechanics: the train with the locomotive; the machinery with the engine; the electrical mechanism with the power house. In the body: the arm with the socket; the brain with the heart. In the christian life the follower of Jesus with the Spirit of Jesus. We have been talking together about making connections, and I believe some of us have made the vital connection this hour, which means new inflow and outflow of power.

Now there will be time for only a brief word about *breaking* connections. "But," you say, "we do not want to break connections." No, *you* do not. But there is someone else who does. Since you have put yourself into intimate contact with Jesus this someone else has become intensely interested in breaking that contact. And this enemy of ours, this Satan, the hater, is subtle and deep and experienced and more than a match for any of us. But greater is He that is now in you than he that is in the world. Satan will do his best by bold attack and cunning deceit to tamper with your couplings.

One of the saddest sights, and yet a not uncommon one, is to see a man who has been mightily used of God, but whose usefulness is now wholly gone. One can run back through only recent years and recall, one after another, those through whom multitudes were blessed, but who, yielding to some subtle temptation, have utterly and forever lost their opportunity of service. The same is true of scores in more secluded circles whose lives, spiritually blighted and dwarfed, tell the same sad story.

These recent instances are but repetitions of older ones. Three times the writer of Judges tells of Samson that "the spirit of the Lord came mightily upon him," and then is added the pathetic sentence —"but he wist not that the Lord was departed from him." And between the two occurs the story of an act of disobedience. Twice the same thing is recorded of King Saul, "the spirit of God came mightily upon him," and the same sequel follows, "the spirit of the Lord had departed." And between the two is found an act of disobedience to

God's command. The ninth of Luke tells a similar story. The disciples had been given power; had used the power for others; were requested to relieve a demonized boy; had tried to; had expected to; but utterly failed, to their own chagrin, and the father's disappointment, amid the surprise and criticism of the crowd. The Master explains that a slipshod connection with God was at the bottom of their failure. Power is not stored in us apart from God's presence. It merely passes through as He has sway. Once the connection between Him and you is disturbed, the flow of power is interrupted. We do not run on the storage battery plan, but on the trolley plan. Constant communication with the source of power is absolutely essential. The spirit of God never leaves us. We do not lose His presence. But whatever grieves Him prevents His presence being manifest. The *evidence* of His presence may be lost through wrongdoing. So I want to give you in very brief compass *the three laws* of the life of power—continued and increasing power. I wish some one had given them to me long ago. It might have saved me many a bad break.

The first law can be put in a single word—*obey*. Obedience is the great foundation law of the christian life. Indeed it is the common fundamental law of all organization, in nature, in military, naval, commercial, political and domestic circles. Obedience is the great essential to securing the purpose of life. Disobedience means disaster. If you turn to scripture you must read almost every page if you would get all the statements and illustrations of obedience and its opposite. Begin with the third of Genesis, where the first disastrous act of disobedience brought a ruin still going on. Run through the three wilderness books, where the new nation is grouped about the smoking mountain. Listen in Deuteronomy to the old man Moses talking during the thirty days' conference they had in Moab's plains before he was taken away. Then into Joshua's book of victory and the Judges' dark story of defeats, through the kingdom books, and the prophecies, and you will find the changes rung more frequently upon *obedience* than anything else. The same is true of the New Testament clear to the last column of the last page.

The fact is, every heart is a battlefield whose possession is being hotly contested. If Jesus is in possession Satan is trying his best by storm or strategy to get in. If Satan be in possession whether as a coarse or a cultured Satan, then Jesus is lovingly storming the door. Satan *can* not get in without your consent, and Jesus *will n*ot. An act of obedience to God is slamming the door in Satan's face, and opening it wider for Jesus' control. Listen with your heart! An act of disobedience, however slight, as *you* think, is slamming the door of your heart in Jesus' face and flinging it open to Satan's entrance. Is that mere rhetoric? It is cold fact. No, it is hot fact. The first great simple law is obedience.

But someone asks, "How shall I know what— whom, to obey? Sometimes the voices coming to my ear seem to be jarring voices; they do not agree. Pastors do not all agree: churches are not quite agreed on some matters: my best friends think differently: how shall I know?" Here comes in *the second law, Obey the book of God as interpreted by the Spirit of God.* Not the book alone. That will lead into superstition. Not to say the Spirit without the book He has indited. That will lead to fanaticism. But the book as interpreted by the Spirit, and the Spirit as He speaks through His book. There is a voice of God, and a Spirit of God and a book of God. God speaks by His Spirit through His word. Sometimes He speaks directly without the written word. But *very, very rarely.* The mental impressions by which the Spirit guides are frequent. But I am speaking now, not of that but of His audible inner voice. He is chary in the use of that. And when he so speaks the *test* is that, of necessity, the voice of God always agrees with itself. The spoken word is never out of harmony with the written word. And as He has given us the written word, it becomes our standard of His will. This book of God was inspired. It *is* inspired. God spoke in it. He speaks in it to-day. You will be surprised to find how light on every sort of question will come through this in-Spirited book.

But someone with a practical turn of mind is thinking: "but it is such a big book. I do not know much about it. I read the psalms some, and some chapters in Isaiah, and the gospels and some in the epistles, but I have no grasp of the whole book; and your second law seems a little beyond me." Then *you* listen to the third law, namely: *time alone with the book daily.* It should be unhurried time. Time enough not to think about time. At least a half hour every day, I would suggest, and preferably the first half hour of the morning, rising at least early enough to get this bit of time before any duty can claim you. It may seem very difficult for some. But it is an absolute essential, for the first two laws depend on this one for their practical force.

When Joshua, trembling, was called upon to assume the stupendous task of being Moses' successor, God came and had a quiet talk with him. In that talk He emphasized just one thing as the secret of his new leadership. Listen: "This book of the law shall not depart out of thy mouth, but thou shalt meditate therein day and night, that thou mayest observe to do according to all that is written therein." There are the three laws straight from the lips of God, packed into a single sentence.

Let us plan to get alone with the Master daily over His word, with the door shut, other things shut out, and ourselves shut in, that we may learn His will, and get strength to do it. And when in doubt *wait*.

The Flood-Tide
of Power

A flood-tide is a rising tide. It flows in and fills up
and spreads out. Wherever it goes it cleanses and
fertilizes and beautifies. For untold centuries Egypt
has depended for its very life upon the yearly
flood-tide of the Nile. The rich bottom lands of the
Connecticut Valley are refertilized every spring by
that river's flood-tide. The green beauty and rich
fruitage of some parts of the Sacramento Valley,
whose soil is flooded by the artificial irrigation-
rivers, are in sharp contrast with adjoining un-
watered portions.

The flood-tide is caused by influences from
above. In the ocean and the portions of rivers under
its influence by the heavenly bodies. In the rivers
by the fall of rain and snow swelling successively
the upper streams and lakes.

God's highest ideal for men is frequently ex-
pressed under the figure of a river running at flood-

143

tide. Ezekiel's vision of the future capital of Israel
gives prominence to a wonderful river gradually
reaching flood-tide and exerting untold influence.

John's companion vision of the future church in
the closing chapters of Revelation finds its radiat-
ing center is an equally wonderful river of water
of life. When Jesus would give a picture of a christian man up to His ideal He exclaims, "Out of his
belly shall flow rivers of living water." John's explanation years after was that He was speaking of
the Holy Spirit's presence in the human life. Jesus'
ideal would put our lives at the flood-tide. No ebb-
tide there. No rise and fall. But a constant flowing
in and filling up and flooding out.

Love is ambitious. God is love. And therefore
God is ambitious for us. In the best sense of the
word He is ambitious for our lives. The old impression has been that salvation is for the soul, and
for heaven. Well it *is* for the soul, and it is for
heaven, but it is for the present life and for this
earth. Some of God's most far-reaching plans have
to do with this earth. To-night we want to get a
glimpse of God's ambitious ideal for our lives
down here; something of an understanding of the
results of the unrestrained presence within us of
His Holy Spirit.

It is not surprising that there have been some
mistaken ideas about the results. It has been a
common supposition that somehow the baptism of
the Holy Spirit is always connected with an evangelistic gift and, further, connected with marked
success in soul-winning. Men have thought of Mr.
Moody facing great crowds, who were swayed and

melted at his words, and of people in great multitudes accepting Christ. Probably the world has never had a finer illustration of a Spirit-filled man than in dear old Moody. And it is not to be wondered at that the rare evangelistic gift of service with which he was endowed and the great results attending it should be so closely allied in our minds with the Spirit-filled life which he exemplified so unusually. In sharp contrast however with that conception will you note that we are told over here in Exodus of a man named Bezalel [1] who was filled with the Spirit of God that he might have skill in carpentry, in metal working, and weaving of fine fabrics, for the construction of the old tent of God. Will you note further that a company of seventy men [2] were filled in a like manner that they might be skilled in conducting the business affairs of the nation; and that Luke tells of Elizabeth [3] being filled that she might become a true mother for John.

A second misconception has been that marked success always accompanies the Spirit's control. In contrast with that will you please note the results in some of the Spirit-swayed men whom God used in Bible times. Isaiah was called to a service that was to be barren of results, though long continued; and Jeremiah's was not only fruitless but with great personal peril. Jesus' public work led through a rough path to a crown of thorns and a cross. Stephen's testimony brought him a storm of

[1] Exodus xxxi: 1–5.
[2] Numbers xi: 16, 17.
[3] Luke i: 13–17, 41.

stones. And Paul passed through great danger and distress to a cell, and beyond, a keen-edged ax. These are leaders among Spirit-filled men.

Paul's teaching in the Corinthian epistle helps one to a clear understanding about results. He explains that while it is one Spirit dwelling in all who acknowledge Jesus as Lord, yet the *evidence* of His presence differs widely in different persons. It is one God working all things in all persons, but with great variety in the gifts bestowed, in the service with which they are intrusted, and in the inner experiences they are conscious of.[1]

What results then may be expected to follow the filling of the Holy Spirit? It may be said in a sentence that Jesus fills us with the same Spirit that filled Himself that He may work out in us His own image and ideal, *and* make use of us in His passionate reaching out after others. If we attempt to analyze these results we shall find them falling into three groups. First—results in the *life,* that is in the inner experiences, and the habits. Second— results in the *personality,* that is in the appearance, and the mental faculties. Third—results in *service.* Let us look a little at each of these.

A Transfigured Life

First regarding the inner experiences. Without doubt the first result experienced will be a new sense of *peace;* a glad, quiet stillness of spirit which nothing seems able to disturb. The heart will be filled with a peace still as the stars, calm as the night, deep as the sea, fragrant as the flowers.

[1] 1 Corinthians xii:1–11.

How many thousands of lips have lovingly lingered over those sweet strong words: "The peace of God, which passeth all understanding, shall guard your heart and thought in Christ Jesus." It is God's peace. It acts as an armed guard drawn up around heart and thoughts to keep unrest out. It is too subtle for intellectual analysis, but it steals into and steadies the heart. You cannot understand it but you can feel it. You cannot get hold of it with your head, but you can with your heart. You do not get it. It gets you. You need not understand in order to experience. Blessed are they that have not understood and yet have yielded and experienced.

> "Peace beginning to be
>   Deep as the sleep of the sea
> When the stars their faces glass
>   In its blue tranquillity:
> Hearts of men upon earth
> That rested not from their birth
> To rest, as the wild waters rest,
> With the colors of heaven on their breast."

With that will come a new intense longing to do the Master's will; to *please Him*. As the days come and go this will come to be the master-passion of this new life. It will drive one with a new purpose and zest to studying the one look which tells His will. That book becomes literally the book of books to the Spirit-dominated man.

With that will come a new desire to talk with this new Master, who talks to you in His word, and is ever at your side sympathetically listening. His book reveals Himself. And better acquaintance with Him will draw you oftener aside for a quiet talk. The *pleasure* of praying will grow by leaps and bounds. Nothing so inspires to prayer as reverent listening to His voice. Frequent use of the ears will result in more frequent use of the voice in prayer and praise. And more: Prayer will come to be a part of service. Intercession will become the life mission.

But I must be frank enough to tell you of another result, which is as sure to come as these— *there will be conflict.* You will be tempted more than ever. Temptations will come with the subtlety of a snake; with the rush of a storm; with the unexpected swiftness of a lightning flash. You see the act of surrender to Jesus is a notice of fight to another. You have changed masters, and the discarded master does not let go easily. He is a trained, toughened fighter. You will think that you never had so many temptations, so strong, so subtle, so trying, so unexpected. But listen—*there will be victory!* Truth goes in pairs. You will be tempted. The devil will attend to that. That is one truth. Its companion truth is this: you will be victorious over temptation as the new Master has sway. Your new Master will attend to that. Great and cunning and strong is the tempter. Do not underrate him. But greater is He that is in you. You cannot overrate Him. He got the victory at every turn during those thirty-three years, and will get it for you as many years and turns as shall make out the span of your life. Your one business will be to let Him have full control.

Still another result, of the surprising sort, will be a new feeling about *sin.* There will be an increased and increasing *sensitiveness* to sin. It will seem so hateful whether coarse or cultured. You will shrink from contact with it. There will also be a growing sense of the *sinfulness* of that old heart of yours, even while you may be having constant victory over temptation. Then, too, there will grow up a yearning, oh! such a heart-yearning as cannot be told in words, *to be pure*, really pure in heart.

A seventh result will be an intense desire to get others to know your wonderful Master. A desire so strong, gripping you so tremendously, that all thought of sacrifice will sink out of sight in its achievement. He is such a Master! so loving, so kind, so wondrous! And so many do not know Him: have wrong ideas about Him. If they only *knew* Him—that surely would settle it. And probably these two—the desire to please Him, and the desire to get others to know Him will take the *mastery* of your ambition and life.

The All-Inclusive Passion

But all of these and much more is included in one of Paul's packed phrases which may be read, "the *love* of God hath *flooded* our hearts through the Holy Spirit given unto us." [1] The all-inclusive result is *love*. That marvelous tender passion—the love of God—heightless, depthless, shoreless, shall *flood* our hearts, making us as gentle and tender-hearted and self-sacrificing and gracious as He. Every phase of life will become a phase of love. Peace is love resting. Bible study is love reading its lover's letters. Prayer is love keeping tryst. Conflict with sin is love jealously fighting for its Lover.

[1] Rom. v:5.

Hatred of sin is love shrinking from that which separates from its lover. Sympathy is love tenderly feeling. Enthusiasm is love burning. Hope is love expecting. Patience is love waiting. Faithfulness is love sticking fast. Humility is love taking its true place. Modesty is love keeping out of sight. Soul-winning is love pleading.

Love is revolutionary. It radically changes us, and revolutionizes our spirit toward all others. Love is democratic. It ruthlessly levels all class distinctions. Love is intensely practical. It is always hunting something to do. Paul lays great stress on this outer practical side. Do you remember his "fruit of the Spirit"? [1] It is an analysis of love. While the first three—"love, joy, peace"—are emotions within, the remaining six are outward toward others. Notice, "long-suffering, gentleness, goodness, faithfulness, meekness," and then the climax is reached in the last—"self-control." And in his great love passage in the first Corinthian epistle,[2] he picks out four of these last six, and shows further just what he means by love in its practical working in the life. "Love-suffering" is repeated, and so is "kindness" or "goodness." "Faithfulness" is reproduced in "never faileth." Then "self-control" receives the emphasis of an eight-fold repetition of "nots." Listen:—"Envieth not," "boasteth not," "not puffed up," "not unseemly," "seeketh not (even) her own," "is not provoked," "taketh not account of evil" (in trying to help others, like Jesus' word "despairing of no man" [3]), "rejoiceth not in

[1] Gal. v:22–23.
[2] 1 Cor. xiii.
[3] Luke vi:35. R. V., margin.

unrighteousness" (that is when the unrighteous is punished, but instead feels sorry for him). What tremendous power of self-mastery in those "nots"! Then the positive side is brought out in four "alls"; two of them—the first and last—passive qualities, "beareth all things," "endureth all things." And in between, two active "hopeth all things," "believeth all things." The passive qualities doing sentinel duty on both sides of the active. These passive traits are intensely active in their passivity. There is a busy time under the surface of those "nots" and "alls." What a wealth of underlying power they reveal! Sometimes folks think it sentimental to talk of love. Probably it is of some stuff that shuffles along under that name. But when the Holy Spirit talks about it, and fills our hearts with it there is seen to be an intensely practical passion at work.

Love is not only the finest fruit, but it is the final test of a christian life. How many splendid men of God have seemed to lack here. What a giant of faith and strength Elijah was. Such intense indignation over sin! Such fearless denunciation! What tremendous faith gripping the very heavens! What marvelous power in prayer. Yet listen to him criticising the faithful remnant whom God lovingly defends against his aspersions. There seems a serious lack there. God seems to understand his need. He asks him to slip down to Horeb for a new vision of his Master. And then He revealed Himself not in whirlwind nor earthquake nor lightning. He doubtless felt at home among these tempestuous outbreaks. They suit his temper. But something startlingly new came to him in that exquisite "sound of gentle stillness," hushing, awing, mellowing, giving a new conception of the dominant heart of his God. Some of us might well drop things, and take a run down to Horeb.

I know an earnest scholarly minister with strong personality, and fearless in his preaching against sin, but who seems to lack this spirit of love. He is so cuttingly critical at times. The other ministers of his town whom he might easily lead, shy off from him. There is no magnetism in the edge of a razor. His critical spirit can be felt when his lips are shut. I recall a woman, earnest, winsome when she chooses to be, an intelligent Bible student, keen-scented for error, a generous giver, but what a sharp edge her tongue has. One is afraid to get close lest it may cut.

When the Holy Spirit takes possession there is *love*, aye, more, a *flood* of love. Have you ever seen a flood? I remember one in the Schuylkill during my boyhood days and how it impressed me. Those who live along the valley of that treacherous mountain stream, the Ohio, know something of the power of a flood. How the waters come rushing down, cutting out new channels, washing down rubbish, tearing valuable property from its moorings, ruling the valley autocratically while men stand back entirely helpless.

Would you care to have a flood-tide of love flush the channelways of your life like that? It would clean out something you have preferred keeping. It would with quiet, ruthless strength, tear some prized possessions from their moorings and send them adrift down stream and out. Its high waters would put out some of the fires on the lower levels.

Better think a bit before opening the sluice-ways for that flood. But ah! it will sweeten and make fragrant. It will cut new channels, and broaden and deepen old ones. And what a harvest will follow in its wake. Floods are apt to do peculiar things. So does this one. It washes out the friction-grit from between the wheels. It does not dull the edge of the tongue, but washes the bitter out of the mouth, and the green out of the eye. It leaves one deaf and blind in some matters, but much keener-sighted and quicker-eared in others. Strange flood that! Would that we all knew more of it.

THE FULLNESS OF THE STATURE OF A MAN

Now note some of the changes *in the personality* which attend the Spirit's unrestrained presence. Without doubt the face will change, though it might be difficult to describe the change. That Spirit within changes the look of the eye. His peace within the heart will affect the flow of blood in the physical heart, and so in turn the clearness of the complexion. The real secret of winsome beauty is here. That new dominant purpose will modulate the voice, and the whole expression of the face, and the touch of the hand, and the carriage of the body. And yet the one changed will be least conscious of it, if conscious at all. Neither Moses nor Stephen knew of their transfigured faces.

It is of peculiar interest to note the changes in the mental make-up. It may be said positively that *the original group of mental faculties remain the same.* There seems to be nothing to indicate that any change takes place in one's natural endowment. No faculty is added that nature had not put there, and certainly none removed.

But it is very clear that there is *a marked development* of these natural gifts, and that this change is brought about by the putting in of a *new and tremendous motive power,* which radically affects everything it touches.

Regarding this development four facts may be noted.

First fact:—*Those faculties or talents which may hitherto have lain latent, unmatured, are aroused into use.* Most men have large undeveloped resources, and endowments. Many of us are one-sided in our development. We are strangers to the real possible self within, unconscious of some of the powers with which we are endowed and intrusted. The Holy Spirit, when given a free hand, works out the fullness of the life that has been put in. The change will not be in the sort but in the size, and that not by an addition but by a growth of what is there.

Moses complains that he is slow of speech and of a slow tongue. God does not promise a new tongue but that he will be *with* him and *train* his tongue. Listen to him forty years after in the Moab Plains, as with brain fired, and tongue loosened and trained he gives that series of farewell talks fairly burning with eloquence. Students of oratory can find no nobler specimens than Deuteronomy furnishes. The unmatured powers lying dormant had been aroused to full growth by the indwelling Spirit of God.

Saintly Dr. A. J. Gordon, whose face was as surely transfigured as was Moses' or Stephen's, used to say that in his earlier years he had no executive ability. Men would say of him, "Well, Gordon can preach but—" intimating that he could not do much else; not much of the practical getting of things done in his makeup. When he was offered the chairmanship of the missionary committee of the Baptist Church, he promptly declined as being utterly unfit for such a task. Finally with reluctance he accepted, and for years he guided and molded with rare sagacity the entire scheme of missionary operation of the great Baptist Church of the North. He was accustomed with rare frankness and modesty to speak of the change in himself as an illustration of how the Spirit develops talents which otherwise had lain unsuspected and unused.

The second fact:—*ALL of one's faculties will be developed to the highest normal pitch.* Not only the undeveloped faculties, but those already developed will know a new life. That new presence within will sharpen the brain, and fire the imagination. It will make the logic keener, the will steadier, the executive faculty more alert.

The civil engineer will be more accurate in his measurements and calculations. The scientific man more keenly observant of facts, better poised in his generalization upon them, and more convincing in his demonstrations. The locomotive engineer will handle his huge machine more skillfully. The road saves money in having a christian hand on the throttle. The lawyer will be more thorough in his sifting of evidence, and more convincing in the planning of his cases. The business man will be even more sharply alive to business. The college student can better grasp his studies, and write with stronger thought and clearer diction. The cook will get a finer flavor into the food. And so on to the end of the list. Why? Not by any magic, but simply and only because man was created to be animated and dominated by the Spirit of God. That is his normal condition. The Spirit of God is his natural atmosphere. The machine works best when run under the inventor's immediate direction. Only as a man—any man—is swayed by the Holy Spirit, will his powers rise to their best. And a man is not doing his best, however hardworking and conscientious, and therefore not fair to his own powers, who lives otherwise.

Some one may enter the objection, that many of the keenest men with finely disciplined powers may be found among non-christian men. But he should remember two facts, first, that a like truth holds good in the opposite camp. There are undoubtedly men whose genius is brilliant because inspired by an evil spirit. There are cultured scholarly men, and keen shrewd business men who have yielded their powers to another than God and are greatly assisted by evil spirits, though it is quite likely that they are not conscious that this is the true analysis of their success.

The second fact to note is that no matter how keen or developed a man's powers may be either as just suggested, or, by dint of native strength and of his own effort they are still of necessity less than they would be if swayed by the Spirit of God. For man is created to be indwelt and inspired by God's Spirit, and his powers *can* not be at their best pitch save as the conditions of their creation are met.

The third fact:—*There will be a gradual bring-*

ing back to their normal condition of those facul-
ties which have been dwarfed, or warped, or
abnormally developed through sin and selfishness.
Sometimes these moral twists and quirks in our
mental faculties are an inheritance through one or
more generations. The man with excessive egotism
often carries the evidence of it in the very shape
of his head. But as he yields to the new Spirit dominant within, a spirit of humility, of modesty will
gradually displace so much of the other as is abnormal. The man of superficial mind will be deep-
ened in his mental processes. The man of hasty
judgment or poor judgment will grow careful in
his conclusions. The lazy man will get a new lease
of ambition and energy.

These results will be gradual, as all of God's
processes are. Sometimes painfully gradual, and
will be strictly in proportion as the man yields himself unreservedly to the control of the indwelling
Spirit. And the process will be by the injection of a
new and mighty motive power. The shallow-minded
man will have an intense desire to study God's
wondrous classic so as to learn His will. And
though his studies may not get much farther, yet
no one book so disciplines the mind and deepens
the mind
as that. The lazy man will find a fire kindling in
his bones to please his Master and do something
for Him, that will burn through and burn up his
indolence. The man of hasty judgment will find
himself stopping to consider what his Master would
desire. And the mere pause to think is a long step
toward more accurate judgment. He will become a
reverent student of the word of God, and nothing
corrects the judgment like that.

The self-willed, headstrong man will likely have the toughest time of any. To let his own plan utterly go, and instead fit into a radically different one will shake him up terrifically. But that mighty One within will lovingly woo and move him. And as he yields, and victory comes, he will be delighted to find that the highest act of the strongest will is in yielding to a higher will when found. He will be charmed to discover that the rarest liberty comes only in perfect obedience to perfect law.

And so every sort of man who has gotten some moral twist or obliquity in his mental make-up will be straightened out to the normal standard of his Maker, *as he allows Him to take full control.*

The fourth fact:—*All this growth and development will be strictly along the groove of the man's natural endowment.* The natural mental bent will not be changed though the moral crooks will be straightened out. Peter's rash, self-assertive twists are corrected, but he remains the same Peter mentally. He does not possess the rare logical powers of Paul, nor the judicial administrative temper of James, before the infilling, and is not endowed with either after that experience. John's intensity which would call down fire to burn up supposed foes is not removed but turned into another channel, and burns itself out in love. Jonathan Edwards retains and develops his marvelous faculty of metaphysical reasoning and uses it to influence men for God. Finney's intensely logical mind is not changed but fired and used in the same direction.

Moody has neither of these gifts, but has an unusually magnetic presence, and a great executive faculty which leaves its impress on his blunt direct speech. His faculties are not changed, nor added to, but developed wonderfully and used. Geo. Mueller never becomes a great preacher like these three; nor an expositor, but finds his rare development in his marked administrative skill. Charles Studd remains a poor speaker with jagged rhetoric and with no organizing knack, though the fire of God in his presence kindles the flames of mission zeal in the British universities, and melts your heart as you listen. Shaftsbury's mental processes show the generations of aristocratic breeding even in his costermonger's cart lovingly winning these men, or after midnight searching out the waifs of London's nooks and docks. Clough is refused by the missionary board because of his lack of certain required qualifications, and when finally he reaches the field none of these qualities appears, but his skill as an engineer gives him a hold upon thousands whom his presence and God-breathed passion for souls win to Jesus Christ. Carey's unusual linguistic talent. Mary Lyon's teaching gift is not changed but developed and used. The growth produced by the Spirit's presence is strictly along the groove of the natural gift. But note that in this great variety of natural endowment there is one trait—a moral trait, not a mental—that marks all alike, namely a pervading purpose, that comes to be a passion, to do God's will, and get men to know Him, and that everything is forced to bend to this dominant purpose. Is not this glorious unity in diversity?

SAVED AND SENT TO SERVE

The third group of results affects our *service*. We will want to serve. Love must act. We must *do*

something for our Master. We must do *something*
for those around us. There will be a new *spirit* of
service. Its peculiar characteristic and charm will
be the *heart of love* in it. Love will envelop and
understand and pervade and exude from all service. There will be a fine graciousness, a patience, a
strong tenderness, an earnest faithfulness, a hope-
ful tirelessness which will despair of no man, and
of no situation.

The *sort* of service and the *sphere* of service will
be left entirely to the direction of the indwelling
Holy Spirit, "dividing to every man *as He will.*"
There will be no choosing of a life work but a
prayerful waiting till *His choice* is clear, and then
a joyous acceptance of that. There will be no attempt to open doors, not even with a single touch
or twist of the knob, but only an entering of *opened*
doors.

If the work be humble, or the place lowly, or
both, there will be a cheery eager using of the
highest powers keyed to their best pitch. If higher
up, a steady remembering that there can be no
power save as the Spirit controls, and a praying to
be kept from the dizziness which unaccustomed
height is apt to product. Large quantities of paper
and ink will be saved. For many letters of application and indorsement will remain *unwritten.*

The Master's say-so is accepted by Spirit-led men
as final. He chooses Peter to *open* the door to the
outer nations, and Paul to *enter* the opened door.
He chooses not an apostle but Philip to open up
Samaria, and Titus to guide church matters in
Crete. A miner's son is chosen to shake Europe,
and a cobbler to kindle anew the missionary fires of

Christendom. Livingstone is sent to open up the heart of Africa for a fresh infusion of the blood of the Son of God. A nurse-maid, whose name remains unknown, is used to mold for God the child who became the seventh Earl of Shaftsbury, one of the most truly Spirit-filled men of the world. Geo. Mueller is chosen for the signal service of re-teaching men that God still lives and actually answers prayer. Speer is used to breathe a new spirit of devotion among college students, and Mott to arouse and organize their service around the world. Geo. Williams and Robert McBurney become the leaders, British and American, in an in-Spirited movement to win young men by thousands. An earnest woman is chosen to mother and to shape for God the tender years of earth's greatest queen, who through character and position exerted a greater influence for righteousness than any other woman. The common factor in all is the Chooser. Jesus is the Chief Executive of the campaign through His Spirit. The direction of it belongs to Him. He knows best what each one can do. He knows best what needs to be done. He is ambitious that each of us shall be the best, and have the best. He has a plan thought out for each life, and for the whole campaign. His Spirit is in us to administer His plan. He never sleeps. He divideth to every man severally as He will. And His is a loving, wise will. It can be trusted.

A Spirit-mastered man slowly comes to understand that service now is apprenticeship-service. He is in training for the time when a King shall reign, and will need tested and trusted and trained servants. He is in college getting ready for commencement day. That *may* explain in part why some of the workers whom *we* think can be least spared, are called away in their prime. Their apprentice term is served. School's out. They are moved up.

The Music of the Wind Harp

Please remember that these are *flood-tide* results. Some good people will never know them except in a very limited way. For they do not open the sluicegates wide enough to let the waters reach flood-tide. *These results will vary in degree with the degree and constancy of the yielding to the Spirit's control.* A full yielding at the start, and constantly continued will bring these results in full measure and without break, though the growth will be gradual. For it is a rising flood, ever increasing in height and depth and sweep and power. Partial surrender will mean only partial results; the largest and finest results come only as the spirit has full control, for the work is all His, by and with our consent.

In one of her exquisite poems Frances Ridley Havergal tells of a friend who was given an aeolian harp which, she was told, sent out unutterably sweet melodies. She tried to bring the music by playing upon it with her hand, but found the seven strings would yield but one tone. Keenly disappointed she turned to the letter sent before the gift and found she had not noticed the directions given. Following them carefully she placed the harp in the opened window-way where the wind could blow upon it. Quite a while she waited but at last in the twilight the music came:

Like stars that tremble into light
    Out of the purple dark, a low sweet note
    Just trembled out of silence, antidote
To any doubt; for never finger might
    Produce that note, so different, so new:
    Melodious pledge that all He promised should
      come true.

Anon a thrill of all the strings;
    And then a flash of music, swift and bright,
    Like a first throb of weird Auroral light,
Then crimson coruscations from the wings
    Of the Pole-spirit; then ecstatic beat,
    As if an angel-host went forth on shining feet.

Soon passed the sounding starlit march,
    And then one swelling note grew full and long,
    While, like a far-off cathedral song,
Through dreamy length of echoing aisle and arch
    Float softest harmonies around, above,
    Like flowing chordal robes of blessing and of love.

Thus, while the holy stars did shine
    And listen, the aeolian marvels breathed;
    While love and peace and gratitude enwreathed
With rich delight in one fair crown were mine.
    The wind that bloweth where it listeth brought
    This glory of harp-music—not my skill or thought.

And the listening friend to whom this wondrous experience is told, who has had a great sorrow in her life, and been much troubled in her thoughts and plans replies:

    ...I too have tried
    My finger skill in vain. But opening now
    My window, like wise Daniel, I will set
    My little harp therein, and listening wait
    The breath of heaven, the Spirit of our God.

May we too learn the lesson of the wind-harp. For man is God's aeolian harp. The human-taught finger skill can bring some rare music, yet by comparison it is at best but a monotone. When the instrument is set to catch the full breathing of the breath of God, then shall it sound out the rarest wealth of music's melodies. As the life is yielded fully to the breathing of the Spirit we shall find the peace of God which passeth all understanding filling the heart; and the power of God that passeth all resisting flooding the life; and others shall find the beauty of God, that passeth all describing, transfiguring the face; and the dewy fragrance of God, that passeth all comparing, pervading the personality, though most likely *we* shall not know it.

Fresh Supplies
of Power

"As the Dew"

There is another very important bit needed to complete the circle of truth we are going over together in these quiet talks. Namely, *the daily life* after the act of surrender and all that comes with that act. The steady pull day by day. After the eagle-flight up into highest air, and the hundred yards dash, or even the mile run, comes the steady, steady walking mile after mile. The real test of life is here. And the highest victories are here, too.

I recall the remark made by a friend when this sort of thing was being discussed:—"I would make the surrender gladly but as I think of my home life I know I cannot keep it." There was the rub. The day-by-day life afterwards. The habitual steady-going when temptations come in, and when many special aids, and stimulating surroundings are withdrawn. This last talk together is about this *afterlife.* What is the plan for that? Well, let us talk it over a bit.

Have you noticed that the old earth receives a fresh baptism of life daily? Every night the life-giving dew is distilled. The moisture rises during the day from ocean, and lake, and river, undergoes a chemical change in God's laboratory and returns nightly in dew to refresh the earth. It brings to all nature new life, with rare beauty, and fills the air with the exquisite fragrance drawn from flowers and plants. Its power to purify and revitalize is peculiar and remarkable. It distils only in the night when the world is at rest. It can come only on clear calm nights. Both cloud and wind disturb and prevent its working. It comes quietly and works noiselessly. But the changes effected are radical and immeasurable. Literally it gives to the earth a nightly baptism of new life. That is God's plan for the earth. And that, too, let me say to you, is His plan for our day-by-day life.

It hushes one's heart with a gentle awe to go out early in the morning after a clear night when air and flower and leaf are fragrant with an indescribable freshness, and listen to God's voice saying, *"I will be as the dew unto Israel."* That sentence is the climax of the book where it occurs.[1] God is trying through Hosea to woo His people away from their evil leaders up to Himself again. To a people who knew well the vitalizing power of the deep dews of an Oriental night, and their own dependence upon them, He says with pleading voice, *"I will be to you as the dew."*

[1] Hosea xiv:5.

The setting of that sentence is made very winsome. The *beauty* of the lily, and of the olive-tree; the *strength* of the roots of Lebanon's giant cedars, and the *fragrance* of their boughs; the *fruitfulness* of the vine, and the *richness* of the grain harvest are used to bring graphically to their minds the meaning of His words: "as the dew."

Tenderly as He speaks to that nation in which His love-plan for a world centered, more tenderly yet does He ever speak to the individual heart. That wondrous One who is "alongside to help" will be by the atmosphere of His presence to you and to me as the dew is to the earth—a daily refreshing of new life, with its new strength, and rare beauty and fine fragrance.

Have you noticed how Jesus Himself puts His ideal for the day-by-day life? At that last Feast of Tabernacles He said, "He that believeth on me out of his inner being shall flow rivers of water of life." [1] Jesus was fairly saturated with the Old Testament figures and language. Here He seems to be thinking, of that remarkable river-vision of Ezekiel's. [2] You remember how much space is given there to describing a wonderful river running through a place where living waters had never flowed. The stream begins with a few strings of water trickling out from under the door-step of the temple, and rises gradually but steadily ankle-deep, knee-deep, loin-deep, over-head, until flood-tide is reached, and an ever rising and deepening flood-tide. And everywhere the waters go is life with

[1] John xii:37–39.
[2] Ezekiel xlvii:1–12.

beauty and fruitfulness. There is no drought, no
ebbing, but a continual flowing in, and filling up,
and flooding out. In these two intensely vivid figures is given our Master's carefully, lovingly
thought out plan for the day-by-day life.

In actual experience the reverse of this is, shall
I say too much if I say, *most commonly* the case?
It seems to be so. Who of us has not at times been
conscious of some failure that cut keenly into the
very tissue of the heart! And even when no such
break may have come there is ever a heart-yearning
for more than has yet been experienced. The men
who seem to know most of God's power have had
great, unspeakable longings at times for a fresh
consciousness of that power.

There is a simple but striking incident told of one
of Mr. Moody's British campaigns. He was resting
a few days after a tour in which God's power was
plainly felt and seen. He was soon to be out at
work again. Talking out of his inner heart to a few
sympathetic friends, he earnestly asked them to
join in prayer that he might receive "a fresh baptism of power." Without doubt that very consciousness of failure, and this longing for more is
evidence of the Spirit's presence within wooing us
up the heights.

The language that springs so readily to one's lips
at such times is just such as Mr. Moody used, a
fresh baptism, a fresh filling, a fresh anointing.
And the *fresh consciousness* of God's presence and
power is to one as a fresh act of anointing on His
part. Practically it does not matter whether there
is actually a fresh act upon the Spirit's part, *or* a

renewed consciousness upon our part of His presence, and a renewed humble depending wholly upon Him. Yet to learn the real truth puts one's relationship to God in the clearer light that prevents periods of doubt and darkness. Does it not too bring one yet nearer to Him? In this case, it certainly suggests a depth and a tenderness of His unparalleled love of which some of us have not even dreamed. So far as the Scriptures seem to suggest there is not a fresh act upon God's part at certain times in one's experience, but His wondrous love is such that there is *a continuous act*—a continuous flooding in of all the gracious power of His Spirit that the human conditions will admit of. The flood-tide is ever being poured out from above, but, as a rule, our gates are not open full width. And so only part can get in, and part which He is giving is restrained by us.

Without doubt, too, the incoming flood expands that into which it comes. And so the capacity increases ever more, and yet more. And, too, we may become much more sensitive to the Spirit's presence. We may grow into better mediums for the transmission of His power. As the hindrances and limitations of centuries of sin's warping and stupefying are gradually lessened there is a freer better channel for the through-flowing of His power.

A TRANSITION STAGE

Such seems to be the teaching of the old Book. Let us look into it a little more particularly. One

needs to be discriminating in quoting the Book of
Acts on this subject. That book marks a *transition
stage* historically in the experience possible to men.
Some of the older persons in the Acts lived in three
distinct periods. There was the Old Testament
period when a salvation was foretold and promised.
Then came the period when Jesus was on the earth
and did a wholly new thing in the world's history
in actually working out a salvation. And then followed the period of the Holy Spirit applying to
men the salvation worked out by Jesus. All these
persons named in the Book of Acts lived both before and after the day of Pentecost, which marked
the descent of the Holy Spirit. The Book of Acts
marks the clear establishing of the transition from
the second to the third of these three periods. Ever
since then men have lived *after* Pentecost. The
transitional period of the Book of Acts is behind us.

Men in Old Testament times both in the Hebrew
nation and outside of it were born of the Spirit,
and under His sway. But there was a limit to what
He could do, because there was a limit to what had
been done. The Holy Spirit is the executive member of the Godhead. He applies to men what has
been worked out, or achieved for them, and only
that. Jesus came and did a new thing which stands
wholly alone in history. He lived a sinless life, and
then He died sacrificially for men, and then further, arose up to a new life after death. The next
step necessary was the sending down of the divine
executive to work out in men this new achievement. He does in men what Jesus did for them. He
can do much more for us than for the Old Testa-

ment people because much more has been done
for us by God through Jesus. The standing of a
saved man before Pentecost was like that of a
young child in a rich family who cannot under the
provisions of the family will come into his inheritance until the majority age is reached. After the
Son of God came, men are *through Him* reckoned
as being *as He is,* namely in full possession of all
rights conferred by being a born son of full age.
Now note carefully that this Book of Acts marks
the transition from the one period to the other. And
so one needs to be discriminating in applying the
experiences of men passing through a transition
period to those who live wholly afterwards.

The After-Teaching

The after-Pentecost teaching, that is the personal
relation to the Spirit by one who has received Him
to-day, may best be learned from the epistles.
Paul's letters form the bulk of the New Testament
after the Book of Acts is passed. They contain the
Spirit's *after-teaching* regarding much which the
disciples were not yet able to receive from Jesus'
own lips. They were written to churches that were
far from ideal. They were composed largely of people dug out of the darkest heathenism. And with
the infinite patience and tact of the Spirit Paul
writes to them with a pen dipped in his own heart.

A rather careful run through these thirteen
letters brings to view two things about the relation
of these people to the Holy Spirit. First there are
certain *allusions* or references to the Spirit, and

then certain *exhortations*. Note first these *allusions*.[1] They are numerous. In them it is constantly
assumed that these people *have received the Holy
Spirit*. Paul's dealing with the twelve disciples
whom he found at Ephesus [2] suggests his habit in
dealing with all whom he taught. Reading that
incident in connection with these letters seems to
suggest that in every place he laid great stress upon
the necessity of the Spirit's control in every life.
And now in writing back to these friends nearly
all the allusions to the Spirit are in language that
assumes that they have surrendered fully and been
filled with His presence.

There are just four *exhortations* about the Holy
Spirit. It is significant to notice what these are *not*.
They are not exhorted to seek the baptism of the
Holy Spirit nor to wait for the filling. There is no
word about refillings, fresh baptisms or anointings.
For these people, unlike most of us to-day, have
been thoroughly instructed regarding the Spirit and
presumably have had the great radical experience
of His full incoming. On the other hand notice
what these exhortations *are*. To the Thessalonians
in his first letter he says, "*Quench not* the Spirit." [3]
To the disciples scattered throughout the province

---

[1] 1 Thessalonians iv:8.
   1 Corinthians xii:1–11.
   2 Corinthians xi:4.
   Galatians iii:2–5; iv:6; v:5, 18, 22–25.
   Romans viii:1–27; xv:13.
   Colossians i:8.
   Philippians iii:3.
   Titus iii:5–6.
[2] Acts xix:6.
[3] 1 Thessalonians v:19.

of Galatia who had been much disturbed by false leaders he gives a rule to be followed, *"Walk* by the Spirit." [1] The other two of these incisive words of advice are found in the Ephesian letter—*"Grieve not* the Spirit of God," [2] and *"be ye filled* with the Spirit." [3]

These exhortations like the allusions assume that they have received the Spirit, and know that they have. The last quoted, "be ye filled," may seem at first flush to be an exception to this, but I think we shall see in a moment that a clearer rendering takes away this seeming, and shows it as agreeing with the others in the general teaching.

This letter to the Ephesians may perhaps be taken as a fair index of the New Testament teaching on this matter after the descent of the Spirit; the *after-teaching* promised by Jesus. It bears evidence of being a sort of circular letter intended to be sent in turn to a number of the churches, and is therefore a still better illustration of the after-teaching. The latter half of the letter is dealing wholly with this question of the day-by-day life after the distinct act of surrender and infilling. Here are found two companion exhortations. One is negative: the other positive. The two together suggest the rounded truth which we are now seeking. On one side is this:—"Grieve not the Spirit of God," and on the other side is this:—"be ye filled with the Spirit." Bishop H. C. G. Moule calls attention to the more nearly accurate reading of this last,—"be ye *filling* with the Spirit." That suggests two things, a *habitual inflow*, and, that *it depends on us* to keep the inlets ever open. Now around about these two companion exhortations are gathered two groups of friendly counsels. One group is about the *grieving* things which must be avoided. The other group is about the positive things to be cultivated. And the inference of the whole passage is that this avoiding and this cultivating result in the habitual filling of the Spirit's presence.

CROSS-CURRENTS

Fresh supplies of power then seem to be dependent upon two things. The first is this:—*Keeping the life clear of hindrances*. This is the negative side, though it takes very positive work. It is really the abnormal side of the true life. Sin is abnormal, unnatural. It is a foreign element that has come into the world and into life disturbing the natural order. It must be kept out. The whole concern here is keeping certain things *out* of the life. The task is that of staying in the world but keeping the world-spirit *out* of us. We are to remain in the world for its sake, but to allow nothing in it to disturb our full touch with the other world where our citizenship is. The christian's position in this world is strikingly like that of a nation's ambassador at a foreign court. Joseph H. Choate mingles freely with the subjects of King Edward, attends many functions, makes speeches, grants occasional interviews, but he is ever on the alert with his rarely keen mind, and long years of legal training not to utter a syllable which might not properly come from the head of his home government. Never for one moment is he off his guard. His whole aim is to keep in perfect sympathy with his home country as represented by its head. He never forgets that he is there as a stranger, sojourning for a while, belonging to and representing a foreign country. So, and only so, all the authority and power of his own government flows through his person and is in every word and act. Such a man invariably provides himself with a home in which is breathed the atmosphere of his far away homeland. Now we are strangers, sojourners, indeed more, ambassadors, representatives of a government foreign to the present prince of this world. It is only as we keep in perfect sympathy with the homeland and its Head that there can flow into and through us all the immeasurable power of our King. Whatever interrupts that intercourse with headquarters interrupts the flow of power in our lives and service. We must guard most jealously against such things.

Electricity helps a man here, in the similes it suggests. For instance the electric current passing into a building is sometimes mysteriously turned aside and work seriously interrupted. A cross-wire dropping down out of place, and leaning upon the feed-wire has drawn the power into itself and off somewhere else. The cross is apt to be in some unknown place, and much searching is frequently necessary before it can be found and fixed. And all the work affected by that feed-wire waits till the fixing is done.

The spirit atmosphere in which we live is full, chock-full, of cross-currents. And a man has to be

keenly alert to keep his feed-wire clear. If it be
crossed, or grounded, away goes the power, while
he may be wondering why.

What are some of the cross-currents that
threaten to draw the power of the feed-wire? Well,
just like the electric currents some of them seem
very trivial. Here are a few of the commoner
ones:—

Failure to keep bodily appetites under control.
Intimate fellowship with those who are enemies of
our Lord, it may be in some organization, or otherwise. The absence of a spirit of loving sympathy.
The dominance in one's life of a critical spirit
which saps the warmth out of everything it touches.
Jealousy, and the whole brood which that single
word suggests. Keeping money which God would
have out in service for himself. Self-seeking. Self-
assertion. A frivolous spirit, instead of a joyous
winsomeness, or a sweet seriousness. Overworking
one's bodily strength, which grows out of a wrong
ambition, and is trusting one's own efforts more
than God's power, and which always involves disobedience of His law for the body. Over-anxiety
which robs the mind of its freshness, and the spirit
of its sweetness, and whose roots are the same as
overwork.

The hot hasty word. The uncontrolled temper.
The pride that will not confess to having been in
the wrong. Lack of rugged honesty in speech. Carelessness in money matters. Lack of reverence for
the body. The unholy use between two, whose relation is the most sacred of earth, of that hallowed
function of nature which has rigidly but one normal use.

Some personal habit which may be common enough, and for which plausible arguments can be made, but which does take the fine edge off of the inner consciousness of the Master's approval. Keen shrewd scheming for position by those in holy service.

Paul's Galatian letter supplies these items:— wrangling; wordy disputes; passionate outbursts of anger; wire-pulling or electioneering, that is, using the world's methods to attain one's ends by those in God's service.

These are some of the cross-currents that are surely drawing the power out of many a life to-day. But how may one know surely about the wrong thing? Well, that One who resides within the heart is very sensitive and is very faithful. If I will jealously keep on good terms, aye on the best terms, with Him, ever listening, ever obeying, I will come to know at first touch the thing that disturbs His sensitive spirit. And to keep that thing *out,* uncompromisingly, unflinchingly *out,* is the only safeguard here.

But there will be continual testings and temptings. Testings by God. Temptings by Satan. There will be testings by God that the realness of the surrender may be made clear, and, too, that in these repeated siftings the dross may all go, and only the pure gold remain. The will must be exercised in rejecting and accepting that its fiber may be toughened. No man knows how deep is the conviction until the test comes. God will test for love's sake to strengthen. Satan will tempt for hate's sake to trip up and weaken. God's testings will give strength for Satan's temptings. And out of this double furnace the gold comes doubly purified.

Some circumstance arises involving a decision.
There is a clear conviction of what the inner One
prefers but it runs against our plans in which
friends or loved ones are concerned who may not
see eye-to-eye with us. To follow the conviction
means misunderstanding and some sacrifice. And
so the test is on. To be tactful, and gentle in following rigidly the clear conviction will take grace, *and,*
will bring a refining of life's strength and fabric.

To run through this old Book and call the names
is to bring to mind the men who have gone through
just such testings and temptations; some with splendid victory, and some with shameful defeat.

So it comes to pass that surrender is not simply
the initial *act* into this life of power. It must become the continuous *habit.* There must be a
habitual living up to the act. Surrender comes to
be an attitude of the will affecting every act and
event of life. And by and by the instinctive measuring of everything by its relation to Jesus comes to
be the involuntary habit of the life.

FRIENDS WITH GOD

The *second thing* upon which fresh supplies of
power hinge is *the cultivation of personal friendship with God.* This is the positive side of the new
life. This is the true natural life. It is the living
constantly in the atmosphere of the Spirit's
presence.

The highest and closest relation possible between any two is friendship. The basis of friendship is sympathy, that is, fellow-feeling. The

atmosphere of friendship is mutual unquestioning trust. In the original meaning of the word, a friend is a lover. A friend is one who loves you for your sake alone, and steadfastly loves, regardless of any return, even return-love. Friendship hungers for a closer knowledge, and for a deeper intimacy. Friendship grows with exchange of confidences. Friends are confidants.

> "As in a double solitude, ye think in each other's hearing."

A man's friendships shape his life more than aught else, or all else.

Now this is the tender relation which God Himself desires with each of us. Did Jesus ever speak more tenderly than on that last Thursday night when He said to those constant companions of two years, "I have called you *friends*, for all things that I heard from My Father I have made known unto you"? Out of his own experience David writes, "The friendship of the Lord is with those that reverently love Him, and He will give evidence of His friendship by showing to them His covenant, His plans, and His power." And David knew. Abraham had the reputation of being a friend of God. He even trusted his darling boy's life to God when he *could not* understand what God was doing. And he found God worthy of his friendship. He spared that darling boy even though later He spared not His own darling boy. It thrills one's heart to hear God saying, "Abraham *my friend*." Friendship with God means such oneness of spirit with Him that He may do with us and through us what He wills.

This and this alone is the true power—God in us, and God with us free to do as He wills.

Now trust is the native air of friendship. A breath of doubt chills and chokes. If one is filled and surrounded by trust in God as the atmosphere of his life his touch with God then becomes most intimate. Satan cannot breathe in that atmosphere. It chokes him. Air is the native element of the bird. Away from air it gasps and dies. Water is the native element of the fish. Out of water it chokes and gasps and dies. Trust is the native element of friendship—friendship with God. A constant feeling of confidence in GOD that believes in His overruling power, and in His unfailing love, and rests in Him in the darkness when the thing you prize most is lying bound on the stony altar.

The Spirit of God is a friend, a lover. He is ever wooing us up the heights. Let us climb up. He is ever wooing us into the inner recesses of friendship with Himself. Shall we not go along with Him? This is the secret of a life ever fresh with the presence of God. It is the only pathway of increasing youthfulness in the power of God.

> "And in old age, when others fade,
>   They fruit still forth shall bring;
>   They shall be fat, and full of sap,
>   And aye be flourishing."

A Bunch of Keys

To those who would enter these inner sacred recesses here is a small bunch of keys which will unlock the doors. Three keys in this bunch; a key-time, a key-book, and a key-word. *The key-*

time is time alone with God daily. With the door shut. Outside things shut outside, and one's self shut in alone with God. This is the trysting-hour with our Friend. Here He will reveal Himself to us, and reveal our real selves to ourselves. This is going to school to God. It is giving Him a chance to instruct and correct, to strengthen and mellow and sweeten us. One must get alone to find out that he never is alone. The more alone we are so far as men are concerned the least alone we are so far as God is concerned. It must be unhurried time. Time enough to forget about time. When the mind is fresh and open. One *must* use this key if he is to know the sweets of friendship with God.

The key-book is this marvelous old classic of God's Word. Take this book with you when you go to keep tryst with your Friend. God speaks in His Word. He will take these words and speak them with His own voice into the ear of your heart. You will be surprised to find how light on every sort of question will come. It is remarkable what a faithful half-hour daily with a good paragraph [1] Bible in wide, swift, continuous reading will do in giving one a swing and a grasp of this old Book. In time, and not long time either, one will come to be saturated with its thought and spirit. Reading the Bible is listening to God. It is fairly pathetic what a hard time God has to get men's ears. He is ever speaking but we will not be quiet enough to hear. One always enjoys listening to his friend. What *this* Friend says to us will change radically our conceptions of Himself, and of life. It will clear the vision, and discipline the judgment, and stiffen the will.

[1] One beauty of the revised version is its paragraphing.

The key-word is obedience: a glad prompt doing
of what our Friend desires *because He desires it.*
Obedience is saying "yes" to God. It is the harmony
of the life with the will of God. With some it seems
to mean a servile bondage to details. It should
rather mean a spirit of *intelligent* loyalty to God.
It aims to *learn* His will, and then to do it. God's
will is revealed in His word. His particular will for
my life He will reveal to me if I will listen, *and,* if
I will obey, so far as I know to obey. If I obey what
I know, I will know more. Obedience is the organ
of knowledge in the soul. "He that willeth to do
His will shall know."

God's will includes His plan for a world, and for
each life in the world. Both concern us. He would
first work in us, that He may work *through* us in
His passionate outreach for a world. His will includes every bit of one's life; and therefore obedience must also include every bit. A run out in a
single direction may serve as a suggestion of many
others.

The law of my body, which obeyed brings or con-
tinues health is God's will, as much as that which
concerns moral action. Our bodies are holy because
God lives in them. Overwork, insufficient sleep,
that imprudent diet and eating which seems the
rule rather than the exception, carelessness of
bodily protection in rain or storm or drafts or
otherwise:—these are sins against God's will for
the body, and no one who is disobedient here can
ever be a channel of power up to the measure of
God's longing for us.

And so regarding all of one's life, one must ever
keep an open mind Godward so as to get a well
balanced sense of what His will is. Practice is the

great thing here. This is school work. By persistent listening and practising there comes a mature judgment which avoids extremes in both directions. But the rule is this: cheery prompt obeying regardless of consequences. Disobedience, failure to obey, is *breaking with our Friend.*

These are the three keys which will let us into the innermost chambers of friendship with God. And with them goes a *key-ring* on which these keys must be strung. It is this:—*implicit trust in God.* Trust is the native air of friendship. In its native air it grows strong and beautiful. Whatever disturbs an active abiding trust in God must be driven out of doors, and kept out. Doubt chills the air below normal. Anxiety overheats the air. A calm looking up into God's face with an unquestioning faith in *Him* under every sort of circumstance—this is trust. Faith has three elements: knowledge, belief and *trust.* Knowledge is acquaintance with certain facts. Belief is accepting these facts as true. *Trust is risking* something that is very precious. Trust is the life-blood of faith. This is the atmosphere of the true natural life as planned by God.

> "If a wren can cling
>   To a spray a-swing
>   In a mad May wind, and sing, and sing,
>   As if she'd burst for joy;
>   Why cannot I,
>   Contented lie,
>   In His quiet arms, beneath His sky,
>   Unmoved by earth's annoy?"

Shall we take these keys, and this key-ring and use them faithfully? It will mean intimate friendship with God. And that is the one secret of power, fresh, and ever freshening.

There is a simple story told of an old German friend of God which illustrates all of this with a charming picturesqueness. Professor Johan Albrecht Bengal was a teacher in the seminary in Denkendorf, Germany, in the eighteenth century. "He united profound reverence for the Bible with an acuteness which let nothing escape him." The seminary students used to wonder at the great intellectuality, and great humility and Christliness which blended their beauty in him. One night, one of them, eager to learn the secret of his holy life, slipped up into his apartments while the professor was out lecturing in the city, and hid himself behind the heavy curtains in the deep recess of the old-fashioned window. Quite a while he waited until he grew weary and thought of how weary his teacher must be with his long day's work in the class-room and the city. At length he heard the step in the hall, and waited breathlessly to learn the coveted secret. The man came in, changed his shoes for slippers, and sitting down at the study table, opened the old well-thumbed German Bible and began reading leisurely page by page. A half-hour he read, three-quarters of an hour, an hour, and more yet. Then leaning his head down on his hands for a few minutes in silence he said in the simplest most familiar way, "Well, Lord Jesus, we're on the same old terms. Good-night."

If we might live like that. Begin the day with a bit of time alone, a good-morning talk with Him. And as the day goes on in its busy round sometimes to put out your hand to Him, and under your breath say, "let's keep on good terms, Lord Jesus." And then when eventide comes in to go off alone with Him for a quiet look into His face, and a good-night talk, and to be able to say, with reverent familiarity: "Good-night, Lord Jesus, we are on the same old terms, you and I, good-night." Ah! such a life will be fairly fragrant with the very presence of God.